Seven Dramatic Moments in the Life of Christ

Plays for Church Events

by

Kenneth S. Barker

JOHN KNOX PRESS
ATLANTA

Dedicated
to my mother and father
who brought me into God's world
and nurtured me in Christian faith.

This collection of chancel dramas grew out of a ministry in Union Church, St. Anne de Bellevue, Montreal. To that congregation and a group of good-hearted amateur thespians under the direction of John Howes, I express my thanks. Without the willingness of the congregation to experiment and the group to work, often on very short notice, you would not have this material in your hands.

The dramas were written for specific settings. "One Came Down at Christmas" and "A Star Led Quest" were presented at Christmas Eve services in place of a sermon. "The Last Meal" and "The Last Word" were similarly presented at Maundy Thursday services. Though the latter would be more appropriate to a Good Friday service we took advantage of the lighting effects made possible in the evening. "A Day on the Soapbox" took the place of a sermon on Pentecost Sunday. And "Fulfilled This Day" was part of a Rally Day service opening a church school year.

However those who use this material should not feel restricted to these settings. The seven acts could be presented as a unit at a special evening service. And the format could vary from a simple "play reading" during a morning service to a more elaborate dramatic production.

In all cases there has been a deliberate attempt to move beyond mere entertainment or mushy sentiment to a thought-provoking portrayal of the Christian gospel.

I should not close without a word of thanks to the officials of John Knox Press for their encouragement and help, and to my wife for her patience with a writing husband.

Kenneth S. Barker
St. Paul's United Church
Orillia, Ontario

Scripture quotations are from the Revised Standard Version of the Holy Bible, copyright, 1946, 1952, and © 1971, 1973 by the Division of Christian Education, National Council of the Churches of Christ in the U.S.A. and used by permission.

Library of Congress Cataloging in Publication Data

Barker, Kenneth S., 1932-
    Seven dramatic moments in the life of Christ.

    1. Jesus Christ—Drama. 2. Church entertain-
ments. I. Title.
PN6120.J35B37   812'.5'4   78-52443
ISBN 0-8042-1432-8

Printed in the United States of America
© copyright 1978 John Knox Press
Atlanta, Georgia

Contents

This book provides a copy of each play for each actor. The pages are perforated so that the pages may be removed and distributed to the cast.

Plays in order of appearance

One Came Down at Christmas
(For three actors)

Though the "look down from heaven" approach has often been used, this one seeks to include some substantial theology in a popular and somewhat humorous vein. Care should nevertheless be taken to control the humor. Raphael should not be allowed to dominate. Michael and Uriel should maintain a sense of realism.

A Star Led Quest
(For eight actors)

Some may find this too somber for a Christmas setting. It is designed to bring out the meaning of Christ's birth against the harshness of life in ancient Palestine and, for many people, today.

Herod, in advanced years, is a mixture of cunning rationality and irrational passion. Gaius is a sycophant who brings out the background and character of the king. The part of Gemellus in his "argument" with Herod should be played with restraint. It is more an attitude of weariness than defiance for he is well aware of the explosive fury of Herod.

Fulfilled This Day
(For four actors)

This act can be used at the beginning of a service in place of the call to worship, opening prayers, and Scripture lesson. In this way the atmosphere of worship can emphasize the traumatic withdrawal of Jesus.

The disturbing, though not abusive nature of his ministry is the theme. The part of Jesus should be played with strong, controlled conviction but not with arrogance, contempt, or belligerence. (The tension should be built up gradually.)

Included in the discussion are elements taken from the baptism, call, temptation, and ministry of Jesus. The act thus bridges the Christmas and Maundy Thursday pieces.

The Last Meal
(For five actors)

Taking the dramatic license of using only four disciples, this act portrays the misunderstanding of the disciples up to and, indeed, beyond the crucifixion.

The format includes elements of the last supper ritual to create an atmosphere of worship, certainly the carefully nourished root of Jesus' ministry.

Care should be taken with the very abrupt denouement. The disciples have been pressing for action. Thinking they have finally received the expected promise, they call for celebration. Against this background the sorrow of Jesus and the betrayal of Judas should be emphasized in the tone of their participation in the last Psalm.

The Last Word
(For five actors)

Divergent attitudes to the death and life of Jesus are expressed by the soldiers at the cross. The coarseness of Marius, the cynicism of Caius and the groping faith of Crispus must be held in sensitive tension.

The most effective conclusion is an abrupt cutting of all lights immediately following the last word. Unfortunately this is difficult on Good Friday morning.

A Strange Meeting
(For four actors)

Though many will readily sense the identity of the Stranger, care should be taken not to emphasize such a possibility. The Stranger should speak and act with detachment. He should neither plead nor upbraid but rather lead the two to their own discovery.

The concluding realization should move from a questioning possibility to a strong conviction, not an easy transition to handle in such few lines.

A Day on the Soapbox
(For four actors)

Peter's defense is presented as a rough and tumble Hyde Park debate. The three bystanders should be located at different points on the chancel stairs facing him.

For dramatic purposes, the full scale conversion in the book of Acts is reduced to a willingness to talk some more. I place no such limitations upon the actual working of God's Spirit.

One Came Down at Christmas

TIME: Immediately prior to the birth of Jesus
PLACE: Heaven
CHARACTERS: Three Angels: The Archangel Michael
                                   Raphael, somewhat rough
                                   Uriel, a little more refined

(Michael comes in with a scroll. He looks about and then commands)

MICHAEL: Uriel!

URIEL: *(snapping to attention)* Here, sir.

MICHAEL: Raphael!

RAPHAEL: Yes, sir.

MICHAEL: I have a special assignment for you. The Lord has decided to send the Son to earth.

RAPHAEL: Where's that?

MICHAEL: It's the third planet in the solar system.

URIEL: The one with Venus and Mars?

MICHAEL: That's the one. We've been there before.

URIEL: But why that one? It's third rate. To say nothing of the way those earth creatures are behaving.

MICHAEL: He's going to **save** them.

RAPHAEL: To **save** them? I wish the Lord wouldn't come up with so many wild schemes to save the universe.

MICHAEL: That's his business, not ours.

RAPHAEL: But this space travel is dangerous. You can get hurt out there. Remember the time we tried to save that fellow from Sodom. What was his name?

URIEL: Lot.

RAPHAEL: Yes. And the time we got those three friends of Daniel out of that fiery oven. I was almost roasted alive.

MICHAEL: You should have followed orders. Only the Son was to go **inside** the furnace.

URIEL: What's the assignment this time?

MICHAEL: You're to go to Bethlehem, a small town in Judea. If you look closely you can see it from here.

RAPHAEL: That place?

URIEL: Doesn't look important to me.

MICHAEL: It isn't. Just a small country town where David lived.

RAPHAEL: I remember him. Good with the slingshot.

MICHAEL: To his credit, he had other skills as well.

URIEL: What about that city a little north of it.

MICHAEL: The Capital? Jerusalem?

URIEL: Yes. It has a palace and some **decent** buildings. **That's** where the Son belongs.

MICHAEL: No! He's not going there. Besides a scoundrel by the name of Herod lives in the palace.

RAPHAEL: Let's move him out then. The boys have been wanting some action. *(He moves as if to leave.)*

MICHAEL: Come back here! No rough stuff! Orders are orders! Bethlehem it is!

URIEL: What are we to do?

MICHAEL: Announce a message.

URIEL: To whom?

MICHAEL: To a group of shepherds who tend their flocks on the hills outside Bethlehem.

URIEL: You must be joking. Bethlehem's bad enough, but shepherds?

RAPHAEL: . . . out on the hills for days without a bath?

MICHAEL: You don't have to get too close.

URIEL: What's the message?

MICHAEL: Quite short. With a little effort you can memorize it. If not, Raphael can hold the cue card.

URIEL: And the message?

MICHAEL: *(unrolling the scroll and reading as a formal proclamation)* Be not afraid! Behold, I bring you good news of the great joy which will come to all the people. To you is born this day in the city of David a Savior, who is Christ the Lord. And this will be a sign for you. You will find a babe wrapped in swaddling clothes and lying in a manger.

RAPHAEL: We'll need the cue card.

URIEL: That's all?

RAPHAEL: You want more?

URIEL: What has a baby's birth to do with the arrival of the Son?

MICHAEL: That's how he's going.

RAPHAEL: Through a womb? How unique!

URIEL: *(with annoyance)* Quiet, Raphael!

MICHAEL: No. For once Raphael's right. He's going to be born as a baby.

URIEL: But they won't **recognize** him. They need a warrior king at least. Preferably some intervention with **angelic force.**

RAPHAEL: Yes. The boys have been doing their battle drill for years.

MICHAEL: There'll be no fighting. THAT'S AN ORDER!

URIEL: Is there anything more to the assignment?

MICHAEL: A Choir. We need a concluding chorus.

RAPHAEL: I don't know about that. We're short on high tenors this year and two of the boys in the bass section are tone deaf.

MICHAEL: We'll have to do with what we've got.

URIEL: Maybe the shepherds will be tone deaf, too.

MICHAEL: That's a thought. Anyway the music critics from Jerusalem won't be there to criticize you. . . . By the way, can you take the organ along?

URIEL: It broke down last week and *(the name of the local organist can be substituted)* is out looking for spare parts.

RAPHAEL: Some of the boys really need that organ.

MICHAEL: Don't worry, Raphael. You're not going to a choir festival. Those hills aren't the best place for close harmony anyway.

URIEL: How does the **chorus** go?

MICHAEL: *(again opening the scroll and reading with emphasis)*
Glory to God in the highest
    And on earth peace among men with whom he is pleased.

RAPHAEL: The "glory of God" I understand. But what does "peace" mean to **those** people?

MICHAEL: Not all are unresponsive to love.

URIEL: Not too many have been responding **lately**.

MICHAEL: I know. And that's the reason the Father has decided to send the Son.

RAPHAEL: He wants more people up here. The parking's bad enough already.

URIEL: I don't know whether we can handle many more.

RAPHAEL: Especially **those** types.

MICHAEL: *(with slight annoyance)* Remember, Raphael, they'll be saved!

RAPHAEL: Yes, sir. But haven't you heard of backsliders?

URIEL: I'm not too happy with their quality, either. Many are ignorant.

RAPHAEL: That means schools.

URIEL: And sick.

RAPHAEL: Hospitals.

URIEL: To say nothing of loose morals.

RAPHAEL: More police.

URIEL: And judges.

RAPHAEL: And prisons.

URIEL: Think of the increased taxation.

MICHAEL: *(interrupting with force)* You forget this is heaven!

URIEL: And I want it to stay that way. These newcomers may lower the quality of life.

RAPHAEL: And the standard of living. The housing values could drop.

MICHAEL: *(again with force)* But these people are redeemed, justified!

URIEL: Aw, sir. You know the Lord. The moment anyone repents, he forgives.

RAPHAEL: Who's to say there aren't phoneys in the bunch.

MICHAEL: *(losing his temper)* LISTEN! We aren't to make that judgment. That's the Lord's job. We announce the birth!

URIEL: And then what?

MICHAEL: Come back!

URIEL: What about the Son? Surely he's going to need **help**?

RAPHAEL: Especially as a baby.

MICHAEL: His parents will take care of him.

RAPHAEL: I hate to leave him there as a helpless infant. What if Herod hears of the birth and tries to kill him?

MICHAEL: I'm sure the Father will take care of that.

URIEL: Will he come back?

MICHAEL: Of course. All humans die . . . eventually.

RAPHAEL: The Son will **die**?

MICHAEL: Everyone who is born dies.

URIEL: He's going to be an ordinary human being?

MICHAEL: Let's say he's going to be a **genuine** human being. He's going to face temptation and suffering and trial and death.

URIEL: That's going **too** far.

MICHAEL: How else could he be truly human?

URIEL: *(with questioning reflection)* It seems a high price to pay.

MICHAEL: The Father and Son have decided no cost is too high.

RAPHAEL: They really must love that world.

URIEL: There must be some less costly way. Why couldn't the Father force those earthlings to return to him . . . without all this suffering?

MICHAEL: Is a person a person without freedom?

URIEL: But being free means you can reject the Lord . . . and hurt other people. . . . What if they refuse the Son?

RAPHAEL: Yes. They could do that. Do you think we should keep the boys on the alert? . . . Just in case?

MICHAEL: No! The orders are that he's on his own.

URIEL: But that could mean his death . . . I mean before he's ready to die . . . and by violence.

MICHAEL: The rumor is that he **will** be killed . . . before he's forty.

URIEL: *(with resignation)* Then he won't have much time to make an impression upon **that** world.

MICHAEL: Uriel, a person's work is measured in the quality of life, not the length of years. The only possible cure is a peace stronger than fear, a mercy more generous than law, a love much greater than hate, a life more powerful than death.

URIEL: Those are moving words, sir. But will they believe what they hear?

MICHAEL: Those words will not only be spoken, Uriel. They will be lived in human flesh, on earth, in the fullness of time. And they will remain on earth through the faithful witness of those who come to know the Son. *(pause)* But hurry off, Raphael. There's a choir to be trained.

One Came Down at Christmas

TIME: Immediately prior to the birth of Jesus
PLACE: Heaven
CHARACTERS: Three Angels: The Archangel Michael
Raphael, somewhat rough
Uriel, a little more refined

(Michael comes in with a scroll. He looks about and then commands)

MICHAEL: Uriel!

URIEL: *(snapping to attention)* Here, sir.

MICHAEL: Raphael!

RAPHAEL: Yes, sir.

MICHAEL: I have a special assignment for you. The Lord has decided to send the Son to earth.

RAPHAEL: Where's that?

MICHAEL: It's the third planet in the solar system.

URIEL: The one with Venus and Mars?

MICHAEL: That's the one. We've been there before.

URIEL: But why that one? It's third rate. To say nothing of the way those earth creatures are behaving.

MICHAEL: He's going to **save** them.

RAPHAEL: To **save** them? I wish the Lord wouldn't come up with so many wild schemes to save the universe.

MICHAEL: That's his business, not ours.

RAPHAEL: But this space travel is dangerous. You can get hurt out there. Remember the time we tried to save that fellow from Sodom. What was his name?

URIEL: Lot.

RAPHAEL: Yes. And the time we got those three friends of Daniel out of that fiery oven. I was almost roasted alive.

MICHAEL: You should have followed orders. Only the Son was to go **inside** the furnace.

URIEL: What's the assignment this time?

MICHAEL: You're to go to Bethlehem, a small town in Judea. If you look closely you can see it from here.

RAPHAEL: That place?

URIEL: Doesn't look important to me.

MICHAEL: It isn't. Just a small country town where David lived.

RAPHAEL: I remember him. Good with the slingshot.

MICHAEL: To his credit, he had other skills as well.

URIEL: What about that city a little north of it.

MICHAEL: The Capital? Jerusalem?

URIEL: Yes. It has a palace and some **decent** buildings. **That's** where the Son belongs.

MICHAEL: No! He's not going there. Besides a scoundrel by the name of Herod lives in the palace.

RAPHAEL: Let's move him out then. The boys have been wanting some action. *(He moves as if to leave.)*

MICHAEL: Come back here! No rough stuff! Orders are orders! Bethlehem it is!

URIEL: What are we to do?

MICHAEL: Announce a message.

URIEL: To whom?

MICHAEL: To a group of shepherds who tend their flocks on the hills outside Bethlehem.

URIEL: You must be joking. Bethlehem's bad enough, but shepherds?

RAPHAEL: . . . out on the hills for days without a bath?

MICHAEL: You don't have to get too close.

URIEL: What's the message?

MICHAEL: Quite short. With a little effort you can memorize it. If not, Raphael can hold the cue card.

URIEL: And the message?

MICHAEL: *(unrolling the scroll and reading as a formal proclamation)* Be not afraid! Behold, I bring you good news of the great joy which will come to all the people. To you is born this day in the city of David a Savior, who is Christ the Lord. And this will be a sign for you. You will find a babe wrapped in swaddling clothes and lying in a manger.

RAPHAEL: We'll need the cue card.

URIEL: That's all?

RAPHAEL: You want more?

URIEL: What has a baby's birth to do with the arrival of the Son?

MICHAEL: That's how he's going.

RAPHAEL: Through a womb? How unique!

URIEL: *(with annoyance)* Quiet, Raphael!

MICHAEL: No. For once Raphael's right. He's going to be born as a baby.

URIEL: But they won't **recognize** him. They need a warrior king at least. Preferably some intervention with **angelic force.**

RAPHAEL: Yes. The boys have been doing their battle drill for years.

MICHAEL: There'll be no fighting. THAT'S AN ORDER!

URIEL: Is there anything more to the assignment?

MICHAEL: A Choir. We need a concluding chorus.

RAPHAEL: I don't know about that. We're short on high tenors this year and two of the boys in the bass section are tone deaf.

MICHAEL: We'll have to do with what we've got.

URIEL: Maybe the shepherds will be tone deaf, too.

MICHAEL: That's a thought. Anyway the music critics from Jerusalem won't be there to criticize you. . . . By the way, can you take the organ along?

URIEL: It broke down last week and *(the name of the local organist can be substituted)* is out looking for spare parts.

RAPHAEL: Some of the boys really need that organ.

MICHAEL: Don't worry, Raphael. You're not going to a choir festival. Those hills aren't the best place for close harmony anyway.

URIEL: How does the **chorus** go?

MICHAEL: *(again opening the scroll and reading with emphasis)*
Glory to God in the highest
    And on earth peace among men with whom he is pleased.

RAPHAEL: The "glory of God" I understand. But what does "peace" mean to **those** people?

MICHAEL: Not all are unresponsive to love.

URIEL: Not too many have been responding **lately**.

MICHAEL: I know. And that's the reason the Father has decided to send the Son.

RAPHAEL: He wants more people up here. The parking's bad enough already.

URIEL: I don't know whether we can handle many more.

RAPHAEL: Especially **those** types.

MICHAEL: *(with slight annoyance)* Remember, Raphael, they'll be saved!

RAPHAEL: Yes, sir. But haven't you heard of backsliders?

URIEL: I'm not too happy with their quality, either. Many are ignorant.

RAPHAEL: That means schools.

URIEL: And sick.

RAPHAEL: Hospitals.

URIEL: To say nothing of loose morals.

RAPHAEL: More police.

URIEL: And judges.

RAPHAEL: And prisons.

URIEL: Think of the increased taxation.

MICHAEL: *(interrupting with force)* You forget this is heaven!

URIEL: And I want it to stay that way. These newcomers may lower the quality of life.

RAPHAEL: And the standard of living. The housing values could drop.

MICHAEL: *(again with force)* But these people are redeemed, justified!

URIEL: Aw, sir. You know the Lord. The moment anyone repents, he forgives.

RAPHAEL: Who's to say there aren't phoneys in the bunch.

MICHAEL: *(losing his temper)* LISTEN! We aren't to make that judgment. That's the Lord's job.
We announce the birth!

URIEL: And then what?

MICHAEL: Come back!

URIEL: What about the Son? Surely he's going to need **help**?

RAPHAEL: Especially as a baby.

MICHAEL: His parents will take care of him.

RAPHAEL: I hate to leave him there as a helpless infant. What if Herod hears of the birth and
tries to kill him?

MICHAEL: I'm sure the Father will take care of that.

URIEL: Will he come back?

MICHAEL: Of course. All humans die . . . eventually.

RAPHAEL: The Son will **die**?

MICHAEL: Everyone who is born dies.

URIEL: He's going to be an ordinary human being?

MICHAEL: Let's say he's going to be a **genuine** human being. He's going to face temptation and suffering and trial and death.

URIEL: That's going **too** far.

MICHAEL: How else could he be truly human?

URIEL: *(with questioning reflection)* It seems a high price to pay.

MICHAEL: The Father and Son have decided no cost is too high.

RAPHAEL: They really must love that world.

URIEL: There must be some less costly way. Why couldn't the Father force those earthlings to return to him . . . without all this suffering?

MICHAEL: Is a person a person without freedom?

URIEL: But being free means you can reject the Lord . . . and hurt other people. . . . What if they refuse the Son?

RAPHAEL: Yes. They could do that. Do you think we should keep the boys on the alert? . . . Just in case?

MICHAEL: No! The orders are that he's on his own.

URIEL: But that could mean his death . . . I mean before he's ready to die . . . and by violence.

MICHAEL: The rumor is that he **will** be killed . . . before he's forty.

URIEL: *(with resignation)* Then he won't have much time to make an impression upon **that** world.

MICHAEL: Uriel, a person's work is measured in the quality of life, not the length of years. The only possible cure is a peace stronger than fear, a mercy more generous than law, a love much greater than hate, a life more powerful than death.

URIEL: Those are moving words, sir. But will they believe what they hear?

MICHAEL: Those words will not only be spoken, Uriel. They will be lived in human flesh, on earth, in the fullness of time. And they will remain on earth through the faithful witness of those who come to know the Son. *(pause)* But hurry off, Raphael. There's a choir to be trained.

One Came Down at Christmas

TIME: Immediately prior to the birth of Jesus

PLACE: Heaven

CHARACTERS: Three Angels: The Archangel Michael
Raphael, somewhat rough
Uriel, a little more refined

(Michael comes in with a scroll. He looks about and then commands)

MICHAEL: Uriel!

URIEL: *(snapping to attention)* Here, sir.

MICHAEL: Raphael!

RAPHAEL: Yes, sir.

MICHAEL: I have a special assignment for you. The Lord has decided to send the Son to earth.

RAPHAEL: Where's that?

MICHAEL: It's the third planet in the solar system.

URIEL: The one with Venus and Mars?

MICHAEL: That's the one. We've been there before.

URIEL: But why that one? It's third rate. To say nothing of the way those earth creatures are behaving.

MICHAEL: He's going to **save** them.

RAPHAEL: To **save** them? I wish the Lord wouldn't come up with so many wild schemes to save the universe.

MICHAEL: That's his business, not ours.

RAPHAEL: But this space travel is dangerous. You can get hurt out there. Remember the time we tried to save that fellow from Sodom. What was his name?

URIEL: Lot.

RAPHAEL: Yes. And the time we got those three friends of Daniel out of that fiery oven. I was almost roasted alive.

MICHAEL: You should have followed orders. Only the Son was to go **inside** the furnace.

URIEL: What's the assignment this time?

MICHAEL: You're to go to Bethlehem, a small town in Judea. If you look closely you can see it from here.

RAPHAEL: That place?

URIEL: Doesn't look important to me.

MICHAEL: It isn't. Just a small country town where David lived.

RAPHAEL: I remember him. Good with the slingshot.

MICHAEL: To his credit, he had other skills as well.

URIEL: What about that city a little north of it.

MICHAEL: The Capital? Jerusalem?

URIEL: Yes. It has a palace and some **decent** buildings. **That's** where the Son belongs.

MICHAEL: No! He's not going there. Besides a scoundrel by the name of Herod lives in the palace.

RAPHAEL: Let's move him out then. The boys have been wanting some action. *(He moves as if to leave.)*

MICHAEL: Come back here! No rough stuff! Orders are orders! Bethlehem it is!

URIEL: What are we to do?

MICHAEL: Announce a message.

URIEL: To whom?

MICHAEL: To a group of shepherds who tend their flocks on the hills outside Bethlehem.

URIEL: You must be joking. Bethlehem's bad enough, but shepherds?

RAPHAEL: . . . out on the hills for days without a bath?

MICHAEL: You don't have to get too close.

URIEL: What's the message?

MICHAEL: Quite short. With a little effort you can memorize it. If not, Raphael can hold the cue card.

URIEL: And the message?

MICHAEL: *(unrolling the scroll and reading as a formal proclamation)* Be not afraid! Behold, I bring you good news of the great joy which will come to all the people. To you is born this day in the city of David a Savior, who is Christ the Lord. And this will be a sign for you. You will find a babe wrapped in swaddling clothes and lying in a manger.

RAPHAEL: We'll need the cue card.

URIEL: That's all?

RAPHAEL: You want more?

URIEL: What has a baby's birth to do with the arrival of the Son?

MICHAEL: That's how he's going.

RAPHAEL: Through a womb? How unique!

URIEL: *(with annoyance)* Quiet, Raphael!

MICHAEL: No. For once Raphael's right. He's going to be born as a baby.

URIEL: But they won't **recognize** him. They need a warrior king at least. Preferably some intervention with **angelic force.**

RAPHAEL: Yes. The boys have been doing their battle drill for years.

MICHAEL: There'll be no fighting. THAT'S AN ORDER!

URIEL: Is there anything more to the assignment?

MICHAEL: A Choir. We need a concluding chorus.

RAPHAEL: I don't know about that. We're short on high tenors this year and two of the boys in the bass section are tone deaf.

MICHAEL: We'll have to do with what we've got.

URIEL: Maybe the shepherds will be tone deaf, too.

MICHAEL: That's a thought. Anyway the music critics from Jerusalem won't be there to criticize you. . . . By the way, can you take the organ along?

URIEL: It broke down last week and *(the name of the local organist can be substituted)* is out looking for spare parts.

RAPHAEL: Some of the boys really need that organ.

MICHAEL: Don't worry, Raphael. You're not going to a choir festival. Those hills aren't the best place for close harmony anyway.

URIEL: How does the **chorus** go?

MICHAEL: *(again opening the scroll and reading with emphasis)*
Glory to God in the highest
    And on earth peace among men with whom he is pleased.

RAPHAEL: The "glory of God" I understand. But what does "peace" mean to **those** people?

MICHAEL: Not all are unresponsive to love.

URIEL: Not too many have been responding **lately**.

MICHAEL: I know. And that's the reason the Father has decided to send the Son.

RAPHAEL: He wants more people up here. The parking's bad enough already.

URIEL: I don't know whether we can handle many more.

RAPHAEL: Especially **those** types.

MICHAEL: *(with slight annoyance)* Remember, Raphael, they'll be saved!

RAPHAEL: Yes, sir. But haven't you heard of backsliders?

URIEL: I'm not too happy with their quality, either. Many are ignorant.

RAPHAEL: That means schools.

URIEL: And sick.

RAPHAEL: Hospitals.

URIEL: To say nothing of loose morals.

RAPHAEL: More police.

URIEL: And judges.

RAPHAEL: And prisons.

URIEL: Think of the increased taxation.

MICHAEL: *(interrupting with force)* You forget this is heaven!

URIEL: And I want it to stay that way. These newcomers may lower the quality of life.

RAPHAEL: And the standard of living. The housing values could drop.

MICHAEL: *(again with force)* But these people are redeemed, justified!

URIEL: Aw, sir. You know the Lord. The moment anyone repents, he forgives.

RAPHAEL: Who's to say there aren't phoneys in the bunch.

MICHAEL: *(losing his temper)* LISTEN! We aren't to make that judgment. That's the Lord's job. We announce the birth!

URIEL: And then what?

MICHAEL: Come back!

URIEL: What about the Son? Surely he's going to need **help**?

RAPHAEL: Especially as a baby.

MICHAEL: His parents will take care of him.

RAPHAEL: I hate to leave him there as a helpless infant. What if Herod hears of the birth and tries to kill him?

MICHAEL: I'm sure the Father will take care of that.

URIEL: Will he come back?

MICHAEL: Of course. All humans die . . . eventually.

RAPHAEL: The Son will **die**?

MICHAEL: Everyone who is born dies.

URIEL: He's going to be an ordinary human being?

MICHAEL: Let's say he's going to be a **genuine** human being. He's going to face temptation and suffering and trial and death.

URIEL: That's going **too** far.

MICHAEL: How else could he be truly human?

URIEL: *(with questioning reflection)* It seems a high price to pay.

MICHAEL: The Father and Son have decided no cost is too high.

RAPHAEL: They really must love that world.

URIEL: There must be some less costly way. Why couldn't the Father force those earthlings to return to him . . . without all this suffering?

MICHAEL: Is a person a person without freedom?

URIEL: But being free means you can reject the Lord . . . and hurt other people. . . . What if they refuse the Son?

RAPHAEL: Yes. They could do that. Do you think we should keep the boys on the alert? . . . Just in case?

MICHAEL: No! The orders are that he's on his own.

URIEL: But that could mean his death . . . I mean before he's ready to die . . . and by violence.

MICHAEL: The rumor is that he **will** be killed . . . before he's forty.

URIEL: *(with resignation)* Then he won't have much time to make an impression upon **that** world.

MICHAEL: Uriel, a person's work is measured in the quality of life, not the length of years. The only possible cure is a peace stronger than fear, a mercy more generous than law, a love much greater than hate, a life more powerful than death.

URIEL: Those are moving words, sir. But will they believe what they hear?

MICHAEL: Those words will not only be spoken, Uriel. They will be lived in human flesh, on earth, in the fullness of time. And they will remain on earth through the faithful witness of those who come to know the Son. *(pause)* But hurry off, Raphael. There's a choir to be trained.

A Star Led Quest

TIME: Approximately 4 B.C.

PLACE: Herod's Throne Room

CHARACTERS: Festus: Herod's attendant
Herod
Gaius: an officer in charge of investigating subversion
Melchior
Balthazar
Caspar
Nicolaus: an advisor, harsh
Gemellus: an advisor, somewhat mellow

FESTUS: *(entering)* Your Majesty, Gaius has arrived.

HEROD: Show him in.

GAIUS: You sent for me, sir?

HEROD: Yes. Sit down. *(a pause)* Some wine?

GAIUS: Please.

HEROD: Festus, some wine for the captain. *(Festus pours out a glass from a container and retires.)* Gaius, I want to discuss the behavior of Antipater. You may remember he's my eldest son by my first wife, Doris.

GAIUS: And logically, your successor.

HEROD: Perhaps. Although my sons Alexander and Aristobulus by my second wife Marianne always considered him a commoner.

GAIUS: But they were executed two years ago.

HEROD: Yes! For plotting treason! But that isn't why I called you, Gaius. I've heard that Antipater was involved in the death of my brother, Pheroras.

GAIUS: The poisoning?

HEROD: That I understand. What concerns me is the possibility he is maneuvering against me.

GAIUS: Why would he do that?

HEROD: With me so near death?

GAIUS: No, your majesty. I meant with Alexander and Aristobulus out of the way.

HEROD: Ah, captain, you forget that I have several other sons who might want the throne. Archelaus and Antipas by Malthace and Philip by Cleopatra.

GAIUS: But they are much younger than Antipater.

HEROD: That means little. Many people consider me a usurper. *(At this point Herod changes tone and bursts out with emotional rage.)* Usurper! I've saved the nation! Restored the economy! Rebuilt the Temple! Solomon did no more! Yet they call me a usurper! *(then in a more subdued tone)* My sons are bred with the same spirit. They wouldn't hesitate to eliminate me, much less a half-brother. I want you to investigate Antipater. If he has been engaged in plots against me, let me know.

FESTUS: *(re-entering)* Your majesty?

HEROD: What is it?

FESTUS: Three men have arrived at the court. They claim to be Wise Men from the East.

HEROD: Do they appear to be men of importance?

FESTUS: No, sir.

HEROD: Then send them on their way.

FESTUS: They seek information about a newborn king.

HEROD: *(struggling to his feet)* A what?

FESTUS: A king. A king of the Jews.

HEROD: Good god! Another claimant to the throne! That's all we need. *(He pauses a moment in deep thought.)* Bring them in at once. *(He painfully seats himself.)*

GAIUS: They might provide some useful information.

HEROD: Yes. Yes. But we must be careful. If we seem disturbed they might become suspicious. We may have stumbled upon another plot.

FESTUS: *(leading in the three Wise Men)* Your majesty, Melchior . . . Balthazar . . . Caspar. *(They bow as their names are called.)* Gentlemen, his majesty, Herod, king of Judea by order of Augustus Caesar, Emperor of Rome.

HEROD: Welcome, sirs. This is Captain Gaius, my attendant. *(Gaius bows to them and they bow in turn.)* I understand you come in search of a newborn king?

MELCHIOR: Yes. It is our understanding that a birth of great significance has taken place and we came to pay our respects to the newborn prince.

HEROD: And who gave you news of this birth?

BALTHAZAR: A star.

GAIUS: A star?

HEROD: Don't be surprised, Captain. You are now in the East where star gazing is an honorable profession. *(turning back to the Wise Men)* And what direction did the star provide?

CASPAR: It led us to Judea. When we reached Jerusalem we naturally thought people would be aware of the birth.

HEROD: Indeed you would. I must offer an explanation for my inability to give you an answer. As you can see I am an old man with little time to live. I had ten wives and many children. My progeny are numerous. Strange as it may seem I am unaware of any expected birth in this large family.

CASPAR: Has there been a birth in, say, the last two years?

HEROD: Why do you ask that?

BALTHAZAR: Because we have been studying the star for that period of time. The prince may be a year or two old by now.

HEROD: I see. And you have no other information? No name or place of birth?

MELCHIOR: None, sir.

HEROD: Gentlemen, I'm as much interested in locating this prince as you are. Perhaps some of my advisors might be able to help. If you'll retire for a few minutes I'll consult them. Festus!

FESTUS: Sir.

HEROD: Show these gentlemen to my private chambers and attend to their wants. And send Nicolaus and Gemellus to me at once. *(They leave and Herod turns to Gaius.)* We may be on to something important.

GAIUS: Could there be a Jewish claimant to the throne?

HEROD: Quite possibly. Many of the more nationalistic Jews have refused to recognize my right to the throne.

GAIUS: But what threat can a child pose?

HEROD: It's not the child. It's those who would use a child to promote rebellion.

FESTUS: Nicolaus and Gemellus, your majesty.

HEROD: Gentlemen.

NICOLAUS: You called.

HEROD: Yes. Come in and sit down. A few moments ago Gaius and I listened to a group of Wise Men from the East. They claimed they had been led by a star to seek a newborn king of the Jews. But they had no information about his identity or place of birth.

NICOLAUS: *(musing)* King of the Jews? They may have inadvertently picked up part of another plot.

HEROD: We've discussed that possibility. I'm sure some are hoping for a Jewish king on my death. Perhaps even before. But I know of no particular family which is making claim to royal privilege.

GEMELLUS: Many Jewish people trace their ancestry back to the Davidic kings.

NICOLAUS: And many expect a restoration of the Davidic dynasty.

HEROD: But would these expectations give a clue to his identity?

GEMELLUS: Not much. The ancient writings are very general in nature.

HEROD: Nothing to indicate his birthplace?

GEMELLUS: There's one which relates to Bethlehem.

GAIUS: Bethlehem?

GEMELLUS: Bethlehem is the ancient city of King David. The passage runs something like this:
　　And you, O Bethlehem,
　　　who are little among the towns of Judah,
　　From you shall come one
　　　who is to be ruler in Israel.

HEROD: It doesn't **say** that's his birth place.

GEMELLUS: No. It's a poetic way of saying that someone of the lineage or spirit of David will come to the throne.

GAIUS: No wonder these people are so unruly.

GEMELLUS: But not all would support an insurrection. Some are more interested in religious or moral renewal. They believe God will send the king when the nation achieves true righteousness.

GAIUS: *(laughing)* That may take some time.

NICOLAUS: Others believe the coming king will be some superhuman, angelic being from heaven.

GEMELLUS: Or the direct intervention of their God.

GAIUS: *(jokingly)* That's tough competition!

HEROD: *(butting in)* Let them dream their dreams. I'm more concerned with the here and now. In the tinder box of the present some group may use a young child as a rallying point.

GAIUS: We don't have much to go on.

HEROD: Only these Wise Men. *(He reflects for a moment.)* I'll call them back, give them this bit of information about Bethlehem and ask them to return when they locate the child. Festus! Bring back the Wise Men. *(Festus leaves.)*

NICOLAUS: But will they return? Wouldn't it be better to torture the information out of them while we have them?

HEROD: I don't think they know any more.

GAIUS: By the time they find the child they may learn that you wouldn't be too favorably disposed to another prince.

HEROD: That's a risk we'll have to take. They may be naive enough to return.

FESTUS: The Wise Men, sir.

HEROD: Come in, gentlemen. Please meet Nicolaus and Gemellus, my advisors. *(They stand and there are bows.)* We have discussed the matter of the young prince. It seems that many Jewish people trace their ancestry back to King David so the new prince might be anyone of that lineage. The only information which might help is a passage from one of their sacred books which refers to Bethlehem, a small village about five miles south of here.

GEMELLUS: The ancient city of King David.

HEROD: In view of my advancing years I am most interested in the matter. If this is the birth of the long promised Messiah, perhaps I could ensure that his claim to the throne receives our closest attention. When you have found him, bring me word that I may come and pay my respects.

MELCHIOR: Thank you for this help. We will continue the search in eager expectation that this birth is of great significance.

HEROD: I assure you it is of very great significance. We will wait to hear from you. *(The Wise Men leave.)*

GAIUS: I hope we've been wise letting them go.

HEROD: Don't worry. I have a contingency plan. The slaughter of all the young children in Bethlehem would certainly discourage any would-be aspirant.

GEMELLUS: *(with a pained, **not** defiant tone)* Good god. Not more bloodshed. Surely we've had enough.

HEROD: That's all some people understand.

GEMELLUS: But there's no proven danger. At worst your sons will quarrel over the succession and Rome will decide. There's no need to slaughter innocent children.

HEROD: If insurrection breaks out Rome will take direct control.

GEMELLUS: Put some of the rebels to death. But not the children.

HEROD: I can't take chances.

GEMELLUS: But we don't know there's a plot. Those Wise Men may be lunatic dreamers.

HEROD: I've learned not to trust anyone.

GEMELLUS: And look at what it's done. Your favorite wife and two sons killed. Your uncle gone.

HEROD: *(in another demented outburst)* But I'm still here! I've survived! I'm still king!

GEMELLUS: But at great cost. Your rule now rests on fear.

HEROD: Any other basis would be futile. Give some of these rebels an inch and they'd take a mile.

GEMELLUS: Surely one can be strong without being brutal. One needn't butcher innocent children. How will people feel about such slaughter?

HEROD: I've long since learned to ignore public sentiment.

GEMELLUS: You have no desire to be loved by your people?

HEROD: No.

GEMELLUS: Respected?

HEROD: They respect power.

GEMELLUS: None to mourn your passing?

HEROD: *(with insidious glee)* I can think of ways to make people mourn my death.

GEMELLUS: You can?

HEROD: Yes. Arrange to have the leading citizens put to death when I die. That will make the tears flow.

GEMELLUS: You must be mad to think such things. Your name will live in infamy.

HEROD: My name will live on as one who held power against great odds.

GEMELLUS: There are moments I think we must all be insane. There must be some better way.

HEROD: The way of those naive Wise Men? Wandering about on some crazy star led quest? Don't be a fool, Gemellus. What are a few more deaths? A hundred years from now no one will remember. The young prince, whoever he is, will be forgotten. The dreams of those Wise Men will still be wild dreams. Men will continue to survive by force as they always have.

GEMELLUS: I'm not trying to be foolish. One must use power to maintain order. But **brute** force staggers from one confrontation to the next.

HEROD: I wouldn't be too hopeful, Gemellus. As long as human nature remains what it is, people will scheme and fight and kill.

GEMELLUS: Unless they learn to struggle for peace and good will. Maybe this is what those old prophets had in mind when they spoke of a coming prince of peace . . . someone not interested in wealth, in fame, in a throne . . . someone only obscure Wise Men will be able to find.

HEROD: *(growing irritated)* Don't try my patience, Gemellus. I've put men to death for less insolence than that. You've been a good friend. I wouldn't want to lose you now. You're not going to change an old man. History will judge me as I am. *(struggling to his feet)* But enough talk for one day. I'm tired. Good night, gentlemen. *(He leaves and the lights, if any, fade. A voice is heard.)*

VOICE: Lo, the star which they had seen in the East went before them, till it came to rest over the place where the child was. When they saw the star, they rejoiced exceedingly with great joy; and going into the house they saw the child with Mary his mother, and they fell down and worshiped him. Then, opening their treasures, they offered him gifts, gold and frankincense and myrrh. . . . And being warned in a dream not to return to Herod, they departed to their own country by another way.

A Star Led Quest

TIME: Approximately 4 B.C.

PLACE: Herod's Throne Room

CHARACTERS: Festus: Herod's attendant
    Herod
    Gaius: an officer in charge of investigating subversion
    Melchior
    Balthazar
    Caspar
    Nicolaus: an advisor, harsh
    Gemellus: an advisor, somewhat mellow

FESTUS: *(entering)* Your Majesty, Gaius has arrived.

HEROD: Show him in.

GAIUS: You sent for me, sir?

HEROD: Yes. Sit down. *(a pause)* Some wine?

GAIUS: Please.

HEROD: Festus, some wine for the captain. *(Festus pours out a glass from a container and retires.)* Gaius, I want to discuss the behavior of Antipater. You may remember he's my eldest son by my first wife, Doris.

GAIUS: And logically, your successor.

HEROD: Perhaps. Although my sons Alexander and Aristobulus by my second wife Marianne always considered him a commoner.

GAIUS: But they were executed two years ago.

HEROD: Yes! For plotting treason! But that isn't why I called you, Gaius. I've heard that Antipater was involved in the death of my brother, Pheroras.

GAIUS: The poisoning?

HEROD: That I understand. What concerns me is the possibility he is maneuvering against me.

GAIUS: Why would he do that?

HEROD: With me so near death?

GAIUS: No, your majesty. I meant with Alexander and Aristobulus out of the way.

HEROD: Ah, captain, you forget that I have several other sons who might want the throne. Archelaus and Antipas by Malthace and Philip by Cleopatra.

GAIUS: But they are much younger than Antipater.

HEROD: That means little. Many people consider me a usurper. *(At this point Herod changes tone and bursts out with emotional rage.)* Usurper! I've saved the nation! Restored the economy! Rebuilt the Temple! Solomon did no more! Yet they call me a usurper! *(then in a more subdued tone)* My sons are bred with the same spirit. They wouldn't hesitate to eliminate me, much less a half-brother. I want you to investigate Antipater. If he has been engaged in plots against me, let me know.

FESTUS: *(re-entering)* Your majesty?

HEROD: What is it?

FESTUS: Three men have arrived at the court. They claim to be Wise Men from the East.

HEROD: Do they appear to be men of importance?

FESTUS: No, sir.

HEROD: Then send them on their way.

FESTUS: They seek information about a newborn king.

HEROD: *(struggling to his feet)* A what?

FESTUS: A king. A king of the Jews.

HEROD: Good god! Another claimant to the throne! That's all we need. *(He pauses a moment in deep thought.)* Bring them in at once. *(He painfully seats himself.)*

GAIUS: They might provide some useful information.

HEROD: Yes. Yes. But we must be careful. If we seem disturbed they might become suspicious. We may have stumbled upon another plot.

FESTUS: *(leading in the three Wise Men)* Your majesty, Melchior . . . Balthazar . . . Caspar. *(They bow as their names are called.)* Gentlemen, his majesty, Herod, king of Judea by order of Augustus Caesar, Emperor of Rome.

HEROD: Welcome, sirs. This is Captain Gaius, my attendant. *(Gaius bows to them and they bow in turn.)* I understand you come in search of a newborn king?

MELCHIOR: Yes. It is our understanding that a birth of great significance has taken place and we came to pay our respects to the newborn prince.

HEROD: And who gave you news of this birth?

BALTHAZAR: A star.

GAIUS: A star?

HEROD: Don't be surprised, Captain. You are now in the East where star gazing is an honorable profession. *(turning back to the Wise Men)* And what direction did the star provide?

CASPAR: It led us to Judea. When we reached Jerusalem we naturally thought people would be aware of the birth.

HEROD: Indeed you would. I must offer an explanation for my inability to give you an answer. As you can see I am an old man with little time to live. I had ten wives and many children. My progeny are numerous. Strange as it may seem I am unaware of any expected birth in this large family.

CASPAR: Has there been a birth in, say, the last two years?

HEROD: Why do you ask that?

BALTHAZAR: Because we have been studying the star for that period of time. The prince may be a year or two old by now.

HEROD: I see. And you have no other information? No name or place of birth?

MELCHIOR: None, sir.

HEROD: Gentlemen, I'm as much interested in locating this prince as you are. Perhaps some of my advisors might be able to help. If you'll retire for a few minutes I'll consult them. Festus!

FESTUS: Sir.

HEROD: Show these gentlemen to my private chambers and attend to their wants. And send Nicolaus and Gemellus to me at once. *(They leave and Herod turns to Gaius.)* We may be on to something important.

GAIUS: Could there be a Jewish claimant to the throne?

HEROD: Quite possibly. Many of the more nationalistic Jews have refused to recognize my right to the throne.

GAIUS: But what threat can a child pose?

HEROD: It's not the child. It's those who would use a child to promote rebellion.

FESTUS: Nicolaus and Gemellus, your majesty.

HEROD: Gentlemen.

NICOLAUS: You called.

HEROD: Yes. Come in and sit down. A few moments ago Gaius and I listened to a group of Wise Men from the East. They claimed they had been led by a star to seek a newborn king of the Jews. But they had no information about his identity or place of birth.

NICOLAUS: *(musing)* King of the Jews? They may have inadvertently picked up part of another plot.

HEROD: We've discussed that possibility. I'm sure some are hoping for a Jewish king on my death. Perhaps even before. But I know of no particular family which is making claim to royal privilege.

GEMELLUS: Many Jewish people trace their ancestry back to the Davidic kings.

NICOLAUS: And many expect a restoration of the Davidic dynasty.

HEROD: But would these expectations give a clue to his identity?

GEMELLUS: Not much. The ancient writings are very general in nature.

HEROD: Nothing to indicate his birthplace?

GEMELLUS: There's one which relates to Bethlehem.

GAIUS: Bethlehem?

GEMELLUS: Bethlehem is the ancient city of King David. The passage runs something like this:
> And you, O Bethlehem,
>   who are little among the towns of Judah,
> From you shall come one
>   who is to be ruler in Israel.

HEROD: It doesn't **say** that's his birth place.

GEMELLUS: No. It's a poetic way of saying that someone of the lineage or spirit of David will come to the throne.

GAIUS: No wonder these people are so unruly.

GEMELLUS: But not all would support an insurrection. Some are more interested in religious or moral renewal. They believe God will send the king when the nation achieves true righteousness.

GAIUS: *(laughing)* That may take some time.

NICOLAUS: Others believe the coming king will be some superhuman, angelic being from heaven.

GEMELLUS: Or the direct intervention of their God.

GAIUS: *(jokingly)* That's tough competition!

HEROD: *(butting in)* Let them dream their dreams. I'm more concerned with the here and now. In the tinder box of the present some group may use a young child as a rallying point.

GAIUS: We don't have much to go on.

HEROD: Only these Wise Men. *(He reflects for a moment.)* I'll call them back, give them this bit of information about Bethlehem and ask them to return when they locate the child. Festus! Bring back the Wise Men. *(Festus leaves.)*

NICOLAUS: But will they return? Wouldn't it be better to torture the information out of them while we have them?

HEROD: I don't think they know any more.

GAIUS: By the time they find the child they may learn that you wouldn't be too favorably disposed to another prince.

HEROD: That's a risk we'll have to take. They may be naive enough to return.

FESTUS: The Wise Men, sir.

HEROD: Come in, gentlemen. Please meet Nicolaus and Gemellus, my advisors. *(They stand and there are bows.)* We have discussed the matter of the young prince. It seems that many Jewish people trace their ancestry back to King David so the new prince might be anyone of that lineage. The only information which might help is a passage from one of their sacred books which refers to Bethlehem, a small village about five miles south of here.

GEMELLUS: The ancient city of King David.

HEROD: In view of my advancing years I am most interested in the matter. If this is the birth of the long promised Messiah, perhaps I could ensure that his claim to the throne receives our closest attention. When you have found him, bring me word that I may come and pay my respects.

MELCHIOR: Thank you for this help. We will continue the search in eager expectation that this birth is of great significance.

HEROD: I assure you it is of very great significance. We will wait to hear from you. *(The Wise Men leave.)*

GAIUS: I hope we've been wise letting them go.

HEROD: Don't worry. I have a contingency plan. The slaughter of all the young children in Bethlehem would certainly discourage any would-be aspirant.

GEMELLUS: *(with a pained, **not** defiant tone)* Good god. Not more bloodshed. Surely we've had enough.

HEROD: That's all some people understand.

GEMELLUS: But there's no proven danger. At worst your sons will quarrel over the succession and Rome will decide. There's no need to slaughter innocent children.

HEROD: If insurrection breaks out Rome will take direct control.

GEMELLUS: Put some of the rebels to death. But not the children.

HEROD: I can't take chances.

GEMELLUS: But we don't know there's a plot. Those Wise Men may be lunatic dreamers.

HEROD: I've learned not to trust anyone.

GEMELLUS: And look at what it's done. Your favorite wife and two sons killed. Your uncle gone.

HEROD: *(in another demented outburst)* But I'm still here! I've survived! I'm still king!

GEMELLUS: But at great cost. Your rule now rests on fear.

HEROD: Any other basis would be futile. Give some of these rebels an inch and they'd take a mile.

GEMELLUS: Surely one can be strong without being brutal. One needn't butcher innocent children. How will people feel about such slaughter?

HEROD: I've long since learned to ignore public sentiment.

GEMELLUS: You have no desire to be loved by your people?

HEROD: No.

GEMELLUS: Respected?

HEROD: They respect power.

GEMELLUS: None to mourn your passing?

HEROD: *(with insidious glee)* I can think of ways to make people mourn my death.

GEMELLUS: You can?

HEROD: Yes. Arrange to have the leading citizens put to death when I die. That will make the tears flow.

GEMELLUS: You must be mad to think such things. Your name will live in infamy.

HEROD: My name will live on as one who held power against great odds.

GEMELLUS: There are moments I think we must all be insane. There must be some better way.

HEROD: The way of those naive Wise Men? Wandering about on some crazy star led quest? Don't be a fool, Gemellus. What are a few more deaths? A hundred years from now no one will remember. The young prince, whoever he is, will be forgotten. The dreams of those Wise Men will still be wild dreams. Men will continue to survive by force as they always have.

GEMELLUS: I'm not trying to be foolish. One must use power to maintain order. But **brute** force staggers from one confrontation to the next.

HEROD: I wouldn't be too hopeful, Gemellus. As long as human nature remains what it is, people will scheme and fight and kill.

GEMELLUS: Unless they learn to struggle for peace and good will. Maybe this is what those old prophets had in mind when they spoke of a coming prince of peace . . . someone not interested in wealth, in fame, in a throne . . . someone only obscure Wise Men will be able to find.

HEROD: *(growing irritated)* Don't try my patience, Gemellus. I've put men to death for less insolence than that. You've been a good friend. I wouldn't want to lose you now. You're not going to change an old man. History will judge me as I am. *(struggling to his feet)* But enough talk for one day. I'm tired. Good night, gentlemen. *(He leaves and the lights, if any, fade. A voice is heard.)*

VOICE: Lo, the star which they had seen in the East went before them, till it came to rest over the place where the child was. When they saw the star, they rejoiced exceedingly with great joy; and going into the house they saw the child with Mary his mother, and they fell down and worshiped him. Then, opening their treasures, they offered him gifts, gold and frankincense and myrrh. . . . And being warned in a dream not to return to Herod, they departed to their own country by another way.

A Star Led Quest

TIME: Approximately 4 B.C.

PLACE: Herod's Throne Room

CHARACTERS: Festus: Herod's attendant
                Herod
                Gaius: an officer in charge of investigating subversion
                Melchior
                Balthazar
                Caspar
                Nicolaus: an advisor, harsh
                Gemellus: an advisor, somewhat mellow

FESTUS: *(entering)* Your Majesty, Gaius has arrived.

HEROD: Show him in.

GAIUS: You sent for me, sir?

HEROD: Yes. Sit down. *(a pause)* Some wine?

GAIUS: Please.

HEROD: Festus, some wine for the captain. *(Festus pours out a glass from a container and retires.)* Gaius, I want to discuss the behavior of Antipater. You may remember he's my eldest son by my first wife, Doris.

GAIUS: And logically, your successor.

HEROD: Perhaps. Although my sons Alexander and Aristobulus by my second wife Marianne always considered him a commoner.

GAIUS: But they were executed two years ago.

HEROD: Yes! For plotting treason! But that isn't why I called you, Gaius. I've heard that Antipater was involved in the death of my brother, Pheroras.

GAIUS: The poisoning?

HEROD: That I understand. What concerns me is the possibility he is maneuvering against me.

GAIUS: Why would he do that?

HEROD: With me so near death?

GAIUS: No, your majesty. I meant with Alexander and Aristobulus out of the way.

HEROD: Ah, captain, you forget that I have several other sons who might want the throne. Archelaus and Antipas by Malthace and Philip by Cleopatra.

GAIUS: But they are much younger than Antipater.

HEROD: That means little. Many people consider me a usurper. *(At this point Herod changes tone and bursts out with emotional rage.)* Usurper! I've saved the nation! Restored the economy! Rebuilt the Temple! Solomon did no more! Yet they call me a usurper! *(then in a more subdued tone)* My sons are bred with the same spirit. They wouldn't hesitate to eliminate me, much less a half-brother. I want you to investigate Antipater. If he has been engaged in plots against me, let me know.

FESTUS: *(re-entering)* Your majesty?

HEROD: What is it?

FESTUS: Three men have arrived at the court. They claim to be Wise Men from the East.

HEROD: Do they appear to be men of importance?

FESTUS: No, sir.

HEROD: Then send them on their way.

FESTUS: They seek information about a newborn king.

HEROD: *(struggling to his feet)* A what?

FESTUS: A king. A king of the Jews.

HEROD: Good god! Another claimant to the throne! That's all we need. *(He pauses a moment in deep thought.)* Bring them in at once. *(He painfully seats himself.)*

GAIUS: They might provide some useful information.

HEROD: Yes. Yes. But we must be careful. If we seem disturbed they might become suspicious. We may have stumbled upon another plot.

FESTUS: *(leading in the three Wise Men)* Your majesty, Melchior . . . Balthazar . . . Caspar. *(They bow as their names are called.)* Gentlemen, his majesty, Herod, king of Judea by order of Augustus Caesar, Emperor of Rome.

HEROD: Welcome, sirs. This is Captain Gaius, my attendant. *(Gaius bows to them and they bow in turn.)* I understand you come in search of a newborn king?

MELCHIOR: Yes. It is our understanding that a birth of great significance has taken place and we came to pay our respects to the newborn prince.

HEROD: And who gave you news of this birth?

BALTHAZAR: A star.

GAIUS: A star?

HEROD: Don't be surprised, Captain. You are now in the East where star gazing is an honorable profession. *(turning back to the Wise Men)* And what direction did the star provide?

CASPAR: It led us to Judea. When we reached Jerusalem we naturally thought people would be aware of the birth.

HEROD: Indeed you would. I must offer an explanation for my inability to give you an answer. As you can see I am an old man with little time to live. I had ten wives and many children. My progeny are numerous. Strange as it may seem I am unaware of any expected birth in this large family.

CASPAR: Has there been a birth in, say, the last two years?

HEROD: Why do you ask that?

BALTHAZAR: Because we have been studying the star for that period of time. The prince may be a year or two old by now.

HEROD: I see. And you have no other information? No name or place of birth?

MELCHIOR: None, sir.

HEROD: Gentlemen, I'm as much interested in locating this prince as you are. Perhaps some of my advisors might be able to help. If you'll retire for a few minutes I'll consult them. Festus!

FESTUS: Sir.

HEROD: Show these gentlemen to my private chambers and attend to their wants. And send Nicolaus and Gemellus to me at once. *(They leave and Herod turns to Gaius.)* We may be on to something important.

GAIUS: Could there be a Jewish claimant to the throne?

HEROD: Quite possibly. Many of the more nationalistic Jews have refused to recognize my right to the throne.

GAIUS: But what threat can a child pose?

HEROD: It's not the child. It's those who would use a child to promote rebellion.

FESTUS: Nicolaus and Gemellus, your majesty.

HEROD: Gentlemen.

NICOLAUS: You called.

HEROD: Yes. Come in and sit down. A few moments ago Gaius and I listened to a group of Wise Men from the East. They claimed they had been led by a star to seek a newborn king of the Jews. But they had no information about his identity or place of birth.

NICOLAUS: *(musing)* King of the Jews? They may have inadvertently picked up part of another plot.

HEROD: We've discussed that possibility. I'm sure some are hoping for a Jewish king on my death. Perhaps even before. But I know of no particular family which is making claim to royal privilege.

GEMELLUS: Many Jewish people trace their ancestry back to the Davidic kings.

NICOLAUS: And many expect a restoration of the Davidic dynasty.

HEROD: But would these expectations give a clue to his identity?

GEMELLUS: Not much. The ancient writings are very general in nature.

HEROD: Nothing to indicate his birthplace?

GEMELLUS: There's one which relates to Bethlehem.

GAIUS: Bethlehem?

GEMELLUS: Bethlehem is the ancient city of King David. The passage runs something like this:
> And you, O Bethlehem,
>   who are little among the towns of Judah,
> From you shall come one
>   who is to be ruler in Israel.

HEROD: It doesn't **say** that's his birth place.

GEMELLUS: No. It's a poetic way of saying that someone of the lineage or spirit of David will come to the throne.

GAIUS: No wonder these people are so unruly.

GEMELLUS: But not all would support an insurrection. Some are more interested in religious or moral renewal. They believe God will send the king when the nation achieves true righteousness.

GAIUS: *(laughing)* That may take some time.

NICOLAUS: Others believe the coming king will be some superhuman, angelic being from heaven.

GEMELLUS: Or the direct intervention of their God.

GAIUS: *(jokingly)* That's tough competition!

HEROD: *(butting in)* Let them dream their dreams. I'm more concerned with the here and now. In the tinder box of the present some group may use a young child as a rallying point.

GAIUS: We don't have much to go on.

HEROD: Only these Wise Men. *(He reflects for a moment.)* I'll call them back, give them this bit of information about Bethlehem and ask them to return when they locate the child. Festus! Bring back the Wise Men. *(Festus leaves.)*

NICOLAUS: But will they return? Wouldn't it be better to torture the information out of them while we have them?

HEROD: I don't think they know any more.

GAIUS: By the time they find the child they may learn that you wouldn't be too favorably disposed to another prince.

HEROD: That's a risk we'll have to take. They may be naive enough to return.

FESTUS: The Wise Men, sir.

HEROD: Come in, gentlemen. Please meet Nicolaus and Gemellus, my advisors. *(They stand and there are bows.)* We have discussed the matter of the young prince. It seems that many Jewish people trace their ancestry back to King David so the new prince might be anyone of that lineage. The only information which might help is a passage from one of their sacred books which refers to Bethlehem, a small village about five miles south of here.

GEMELLUS: The ancient city of King David.

HEROD: In view of my advancing years I am most interested in the matter. If this is the birth of the long promised Messiah, perhaps I could ensure that his claim to the throne receives our closest attention. When you have found him, bring me word that I may come and pay my respects.

MELCHIOR: Thank you for this help. We will continue the search in eager expectation that this birth is of great significance.

HEROD: I assure you it is of very great significance. We will wait to hear from you. *(The Wise Men leave.)*

GAIUS: I hope we've been wise letting them go.

HEROD: Don't worry. I have a contingency plan. The slaughter of all the young children in Bethlehem would certainly discourage any would-be aspirant.

GEMELLUS: *(with a pained, **not** defiant tone)* Good god. Not more bloodshed. Surely we've had enough.

HEROD: That's all some people understand.

GEMELLUS: But there's no proven danger. At worst your sons will quarrel over the succession and Rome will decide. There's no need to slaughter innocent children.

HEROD: If insurrection breaks out Rome will take direct control.

GEMELLUS: Put some of the rebels to death. But not the children.

HEROD: I can't take chances.

GEMELLUS: But we don't know there's a plot. Those Wise Men may be lunatic dreamers.

HEROD: I've learned not to trust anyone.

GEMELLUS: And look at what it's done. Your favorite wife and two sons killed. Your uncle gone.

HEROD: *(in another demented outburst)* But I'm still here! I've survived! I'm still king!

GEMELLUS: But at great cost. Your rule now rests on fear.

HEROD: Any other basis would be futile. Give some of these rebels an inch and they'd take a mile.

GEMELLUS: Surely one can be strong without being brutal. One needn't butcher innocent children. How will people feel about such slaughter?

HEROD: I've long since learned to ignore public sentiment.

GEMELLUS: You have no desire to be loved by your people?

HEROD: No.

GEMELLUS: Respected?

HEROD: They respect power.

GEMELLUS: None to mourn your passing?

HEROD: *(with insidious glee)* I can think of ways to make people mourn my death.

GEMELLUS: You can?

HEROD: Yes. Arrange to have the leading citizens put to death when I die. That will make the tears flow.

GEMELLUS: You must be mad to think such things. Your name will live in infamy.

HEROD: My name will live on as one who held power against great odds.

GEMELLUS: There are moments I think we must all be insane. There must be some better way.

HEROD: The way of those naive Wise Men? Wandering about on some crazy star led quest? Don't be a fool, Gemellus. What are a few more deaths? A hundred years from now no one will remember. The young prince, whoever he is, will be forgotten. The dreams of those Wise Men will still be wild dreams. Men will continue to survive by force as they always have.

GEMELLUS: I'm not trying to be foolish. One must use power to maintain order. But **brute** force staggers from one confrontation to the next.

HEROD: I wouldn't be too hopeful, Gemellus. As long as human nature remains what it is, people will scheme and fight and kill.

GEMELLUS: Unless they learn to struggle for peace and good will. Maybe this is what those old prophets had in mind when they spoke of a coming prince of peace . . . someone not interested in wealth, in fame, in a throne . . . someone only obscure Wise Men will be able to find.

HEROD: *(growing irritated)* Don't try my patience, Gemellus. I've put men to death for less insolence than that. You've been a good friend. I wouldn't want to lose you now. You're not going to change an old man. History will judge me as I am. *(struggling to his feet)* But enough talk for one day. I'm tired. Good night, gentlemen. *(He leaves and the lights, if any, fade. A voice is heard.)*

VOICE: Lo, the star which they had seen in the East went before them, till it came to rest over the place where the child was. When they saw the star, they rejoiced exceedingly with great joy; and going into the house they saw the child with Mary his mother, and they fell down and worshiped him. Then, opening their treasures, they offered him gifts, gold and frankincense and myrrh. . . . And being warned in a dream not to return to Herod, they departed to their own country by another way.

A Star Led Quest

TIME: Approximately 4 B.C.

PLACE: Herod's Throne Room

CHARACTERS: Festus: Herod's attendant
             Herod
             Gaius: an officer in charge of investigating subversion
             Melchior
             Balthazar
             Caspar
             Nicolaus: an advisor, harsh
             Gemellus: an advisor, somewhat mellow

FESTUS: *(entering)* Your Majesty, Gaius has arrived.

HEROD: Show him in.

GAIUS: You sent for me, sir?

HEROD: Yes. Sit down. *(a pause)* Some wine?

GAIUS: Please.

HEROD: Festus, some wine for the captain. *(Festus pours out a glass from a container and retires.)* Gaius, I want to discuss the behavior of Antipater. You may remember he's my eldest son by my first wife, Doris.

GAIUS: And logically, your successor.

HEROD: Perhaps. Although my sons Alexander and Aristobulus by my second wife Marianne always considered him a commoner.

GAIUS: But they were executed two years ago.

HEROD: Yes! For plotting treason! But that isn't why I called you, Gaius. I've heard that Antipater was involved in the death of my brother, Pheroras.

GAIUS: The poisoning?

HEROD: That I understand. What concerns me is the possibility he is maneuvering against me.

GAIUS: Why would he do that?

HEROD: With me so near death?

GAIUS: No, your majesty. I meant with Alexander and Aristobulus out of the way.

HEROD: Ah, captain, you forget that I have several other sons who might want the throne. Archelaus and Antipas by Malthace and Philip by Cleopatra.

GAIUS: But they are much younger than Antipater.

HEROD: That means little. Many people consider me a usurper. *(At this point Herod changes tone and bursts out with emotional rage.)* Usurper! I've saved the nation! Restored the economy! Rebuilt the Temple! Solomon did no more! Yet they call me a usurper! *(then in a more subdued tone)* My sons are bred with the same spirit. They wouldn't hesitate to eliminate me, much less a half-brother. I want you to investigate Antipater. If he has been engaged in plots against me, let me know.

FESTUS: *(re-entering)* Your majesty?

HEROD: What is it?

FESTUS: Three men have arrived at the court. They claim to be Wise Men from the East.

HEROD: Do they appear to be men of importance?

FESTUS: No, sir.

HEROD: Then send them on their way.

FESTUS: They seek information about a newborn king.

HEROD: *(struggling to his feet)* A what?

FESTUS: A king. A king of the Jews.

HEROD: Good god! Another claimant to the throne! That's all we need. *(He pauses a moment in deep thought.)* Bring them in at once. *(He painfully seats himself.)*

GAIUS: They might provide some useful information.

HEROD: Yes. Yes. But we must be careful. If we seem disturbed they might become suspicious. We may have stumbled upon another plot.

FESTUS: *(leading in the three Wise Men)* Your majesty, Melchior . . . Balthazar . . . Caspar. *(They bow as their names are called.)* Gentlemen, his majesty, Herod, king of Judea by order of Augustus Caesar, Emperor of Rome.

HEROD: Welcome, sirs. This is Captain Gaius, my attendant. *(Gaius bows to them and they bow in turn.)* I understand you come in search of a newborn king?

MELCHIOR: Yes. It is our understanding that a birth of great significance has taken place and we came to pay our respects to the newborn prince.

HEROD: And who gave you news of this birth?

BALTHAZAR: A star.

GAIUS: A star?

HEROD: Don't be surprised, Captain. You are now in the East where star gazing is an honorable profession. *(turning back to the Wise Men)* And what direction did the star provide?

CASPAR: It led us to Judea. When we reached Jerusalem we naturally thought people would be aware of the birth.

HEROD: Indeed you would. I must offer an explanation for my inability to give you an answer. As you can see I am an old man with little time to live. I had ten wives and many children. My progeny are numerous. Strange as it may seem I am unaware of any expected birth in this large family.

CASPAR: Has there been a birth in, say, the last two years?

HEROD: Why do you ask that?

BALTHAZAR: Because we have been studying the star for that period of time. The prince may be a year or two old by now.

HEROD: I see. And you have no other information? No name or place of birth?

MELCHIOR: None, sir.

HEROD: Gentlemen, I'm as much interested in locating this prince as you are. Perhaps some of my advisors might be able to help. If you'll retire for a few minutes I'll consult them. Festus!

FESTUS: Sir.

HEROD: Show these gentlemen to my private chambers and attend to their wants. And send Nicolaus and Gemellus to me at once. *(They leave and Herod turns to Gaius.)* We may be on to something important.

GAIUS: Could there be a Jewish claimant to the throne?

HEROD: Quite possibly. Many of the more nationalistic Jews have refused to recognize my right to the throne.

GAIUS: But what threat can a child pose?

HEROD: It's not the child. It's those who would use a child to promote rebellion.

FESTUS: Nicolaus and Gemellus, your majesty.

HEROD: Gentlemen.

NICOLAUS: You called.

HEROD: Yes. Come in and sit down. A few moments ago Gaius and I listened to a group of Wise Men from the East. They claimed they had been led by a star to seek a newborn king of the Jews. But they had no information about his identity or place of birth.

NICOLAUS: *(musing)* King of the Jews? They may have inadvertently picked up part of another plot.

HEROD: We've discussed that possibility. I'm sure some are hoping for a Jewish king on my death. Perhaps even before. But I know of no particular family which is making claim to royal privilege.

GEMELLUS: Many Jewish people trace their ancestry back to the Davidic kings.

NICOLAUS: And many expect a restoration of the Davidic dynasty.

HEROD: But would these expectations give a clue to his identity?

GEMELLUS: Not much. The ancient writings are very general in nature.

HEROD: Nothing to indicate his birthplace?

GEMELLUS: There's one which relates to Bethlehem.

GAIUS: Bethlehem?

GEMELLUS: Bethlehem is the ancient city of King David. The passage runs something like this:
> And you, O Bethlehem,
>   who are little among the towns of Judah,
> From you shall come one
>   who is to be ruler in Israel.

HEROD: It doesn't **say** that's his birth place.

GEMELLUS: No. It's a poetic way of saying that someone of the lineage or spirit of David will come to the throne.

GAIUS: No wonder these people are so unruly.

GEMELLUS: But not all would support an insurrection. Some are more interested in religious or moral renewal. They believe God will send the king when the nation achieves true righteousness.

GAIUS: *(laughing)* That may take some time.

NICOLAUS: Others believe the coming king will be some superhuman, angelic being from heaven.

GEMELLUS: Or the direct intervention of their God.

GAIUS: *(jokingly)* That's tough competition!

HEROD: *(butting in)* Let them dream their dreams. I'm more concerned with the here and now. In the tinder box of the present some group may use a young child as a rallying point.

GAIUS: We don't have much to go on.

HEROD: Only these Wise Men. *(He reflects for a moment.)* I'll call them back, give them this bit of information about Bethlehem and ask them to return when they locate the child. Festus! Bring back the Wise Men. *(Festus leaves.)*

NICOLAUS: But will they return? Wouldn't it be better to torture the information out of them while we have them?

HEROD: I don't think they know any more.

GAIUS: By the time they find the child they may learn that you wouldn't be too favorably disposed to another prince.

HEROD: That's a risk we'll have to take. They may be naive enough to return.

FESTUS: The Wise Men, sir.

HEROD: Come in, gentlemen. Please meet Nicolaus and Gemellus, my advisors. *(They stand and there are bows.)* We have discussed the matter of the young prince. It seems that many Jewish people trace their ancestry back to King David so the new prince might be anyone of that lineage. The only information which might help is a passage from one of their sacred books which refers to Bethlehem, a small village about five miles south of here.

GEMELLUS: The ancient city of King David.

HEROD: In view of my advancing years I am most interested in the matter. If this is the birth of the long promised Messiah, perhaps I could ensure that his claim to the throne receives our closest attention. When you have found him, bring me word that I may come and pay my respects.

MELCHIOR: Thank you for this help. We will continue the search in eager expectation that this birth is of great significance.

HEROD: I assure you it is of very great significance. We will wait to hear from you. *(The Wise Men leave.)*

GAIUS: I hope we've been wise letting them go.

HEROD: Don't worry. I have a contingency plan. The slaughter of all the young children in Bethlehem would certainly discourage any would-be aspirant.

GEMELLUS:	*(with a pained,* **not** *defiant tone)* Good god. Not more bloodshed. Surely we've had enough.
HEROD:	That's all some people understand.
GEMELLUS:	But there's no proven danger. At worst your sons will quarrel over the succession and Rome will decide. There's no need to slaughter innocent children.
HEROD:	If insurrection breaks out Rome will take direct control.
GEMELLUS:	Put some of the rebels to death. But not the children.
HEROD:	I can't take chances.
GEMELLUS:	But we don't know there's a plot. Those Wise Men may be lunatic dreamers.
HEROD:	I've learned not to trust anyone.
GEMELLUS:	And look at what it's done. Your favorite wife and two sons killed. Your uncle gone.
HEROD:	*(in another demented outburst)* But I'm still here! I've survived! I'm still king!
GEMELLUS:	But at great cost. Your rule now rests on fear.
HEROD:	Any other basis would be futile. Give some of these rebels an inch and they'd take a mile.
GEMELLUS:	Surely one can be strong without being brutal. One needn't butcher innocent children. How will people feel about such slaughter?
HEROD:	I've long since learned to ignore public sentiment.
GEMELLUS:	You have no desire to be loved by your people?
HEROD:	No.
GEMELLUS:	Respected?
HEROD:	They respect power.
GEMELLUS:	None to mourn your passing?
HEROD:	*(with insidious glee)* I can think of ways to make people mourn my death.
GEMELLUS:	You can?
HEROD:	Yes. Arrange to have the leading citizens put to death when I die. That will make the tears flow.
GEMELLUS:	You must be mad to think such things. Your name will live in infamy.
HEROD:	My name will live on as one who held power against great odds.
GEMELLUS:	There are moments I think we must all be insane. There must be some better way.
HEROD:	The way of those naive Wise Men? Wandering about on some crazy star led quest? Don't be a fool, Gemellus. What are a few more deaths? A hundred years from now no one will remember. The young prince, whoever he is, will be forgotten. The dreams of those Wise Men will still be wild dreams. Men will continue to survive by force as they always have.
GEMELLUS:	I'm not trying to be foolish. One must use power to maintain order. But **brute** force staggers from one confrontation to the next.

HEROD: I wouldn't be too hopeful, Gemellus. As long as human nature remains what it is, people will scheme and fight and kill.

GEMELLUS: Unless they learn to struggle for peace and good will. Maybe this is what those old prophets had in mind when they spoke of a coming prince of peace . . . someone not interested in wealth, in fame, in a throne . . . someone only obscure Wise Men will be able to find.

HEROD: *(growing irritated)* Don't try my patience, Gemellus. I've put men to death for less insolence than that. You've been a good friend. I wouldn't want to lose you now. You're not going to change an old man. History will judge me as I am. *(struggling to his feet)* But enough talk for one day. I'm tired. Good night, gentlemen. *(He leaves and the lights, if any, fade. A voice is heard.)*

VOICE: Lo, the star which they had seen in the East went before them, till it came to rest over the place where the child was. When they saw the star, they rejoiced exceedingly with great joy; and going into the house they saw the child with Mary his mother, and they fell down and worshiped him. Then, opening their treasures, they offered him gifts, gold and frankincense and myrrh. . . . And being warned in a dream not to return to Herod, they departed to their own country by another way.

A Star Led Quest

TIME: Approximately 4 B.C.

PLACE: Herod's Throne Room

CHARACTERS: Festus: Herod's attendant
                 Herod
                 Gaius: an officer in charge of investigating subversion
                 Melchior
                 Balthazar
                 Caspar
                 Nicolaus: an advisor, harsh
                 Gemellus: an advisor, somewhat mellow

FESTUS: *(entering)* Your Majesty, Gaius has arrived.

HEROD: Show him in.

GAIUS: You sent for me, sir?

HEROD: Yes. Sit down. *(a pause)* Some wine?

GAIUS: Please.

HEROD: Festus, some wine for the captain. *(Festus pours out a glass from a container and retires.)* Gaius, I want to discuss the behavior of Antipater. You may remember he's my eldest son by my first wife, Doris.

GAIUS: And logically, your successor.

HEROD: Perhaps. Although my sons Alexander and Aristobulus by my second wife Marianne always considered him a commoner.

GAIUS: But they were executed two years ago.

HEROD: Yes! For plotting treason! But that isn't why I called you, Gaius. I've heard that Antipater was involved in the death of my brother, Pheroras.

GAIUS: The poisoning?

HEROD: That I understand. What concerns me is the possibility he is maneuvering against me.

GAIUS: Why would he do that?

HEROD: With me so near death?

GAIUS: No, your majesty. I meant with Alexander and Aristobulus out of the way.

HEROD: Ah, captain, you forget that I have several other sons who might want the throne. Archelaus and Antipas by Malthace and Philip by Cleopatra.

GAIUS: But they are much younger than Antipater.

HEROD: That means little. Many people consider me a usurper. *(At this point Herod changes tone and bursts out with emotional rage.)* Usurper! I've saved the nation! Restored the economy! Rebuilt the Temple! Solomon did no more! Yet they call me a usurper! *(then in a more subdued tone)* My sons are bred with the same spirit. They wouldn't hesitate to eliminate me, much less a half-brother. I want you to investigate Antipater. If he has been engaged in plots against me, let me know.

FESTUS: *(re-entering)* Your majesty?

HEROD: What is it?

FESTUS: Three men have arrived at the court. They claim to be Wise Men from the East.

HEROD: Do they appear to be men of importance?

FESTUS: No, sir.

HEROD: Then send them on their way.

FESTUS: They seek information about a newborn king.

HEROD: *(struggling to his feet)* A what?

FESTUS: A king. A king of the Jews.

HEROD: Good god! Another claimant to the throne! That's all we need. *(He pauses a moment in deep thought.)* Bring them in at once. *(He painfully seats himself.)*

GAIUS: They might provide some useful information.

HEROD: Yes. Yes. But we must be careful. If we seem disturbed they might become suspicious. We may have stumbled upon another plot.

FESTUS: *(leading in the three Wise Men)* Your majesty, Melchior . . . Balthazar . . . Caspar. *(They bow as their names are called.)* Gentlemen, his majesty, Herod, king of Judea by order of Augustus Caesar, Emperor of Rome.

HEROD: Welcome, sirs. This is Captain Gaius, my attendant. *(Gaius bows to them and they bow in turn.)* I understand you come in search of a newborn king?

MELCHIOR: Yes. It is our understanding that a birth of great significance has taken place and we came to pay our respects to the newborn prince.

HEROD: And who gave you news of this birth?

BALTHAZAR: A star.

GAIUS: A star?

HEROD: Don't be surprised, Captain. You are now in the East where star gazing is an honorable profession. *(turning back to the Wise Men)* And what direction did the star provide?

CASPAR: It led us to Judea. When we reached Jerusalem we naturally thought people would be aware of the birth.

HEROD: Indeed you would. I must offer an explanation for my inability to give you an answer. As you can see I am an old man with little time to live. I had ten wives and many children. My progeny are numerous. Strange as it may seem I am unaware of any expected birth in this large family.

CASPAR: Has there been a birth in, say, the last two years?

HEROD: Why do you ask that?

BALTHAZAR: Because we have been studying the star for that period of time. The prince may be a year or two old by now.

HEROD: I see. And you have no other information? No name or place of birth?

MELCHIOR: None, sir.

HEROD:	Gentlemen, I'm as much interested in locating this prince as you are. Perhaps some of my advisors might be able to help. If you'll retire for a few minutes I'll consult them. Festus!
FESTUS:	Sir.
HEROD:	Show these gentlemen to my private chambers and attend to their wants. And send Nicolaus and Gemellus to me at once. *(They leave and Herod turns to Gaius.)* We may be on to something important.
GAIUS:	Could there be a Jewish claimant to the throne?
HEROD:	Quite possibly. Many of the more nationalistic Jews have refused to recognize my right to the throne.
GAIUS:	But what threat can a child pose?
HEROD:	It's not the child. It's those who would use a child to promote rebellion.
FESTUS:	Nicolaus and Gemellus, your majesty.
HEROD:	Gentlemen.
NICOLAUS:	You called.
HEROD:	Yes. Come in and sit down. A few moments ago Gaius and I listened to a group of Wise Men from the East. They claimed they had been led by a star to seek a newborn king of the Jews. But they had no information about his identity or place of birth.
NICOLAUS:	*(musing)* King of the Jews? They may have inadvertently picked up part of another plot.
HEROD:	We've discussed that possibility. I'm sure some are hoping for a Jewish king on my death. Perhaps even before. But I know of no particular family which is making claim to royal privilege.
GEMELLUS:	Many Jewish people trace their ancestry back to the Davidic kings.
NICOLAUS:	And many expect a restoration of the Davidic dynasty.
HEROD:	But would these expectations give a clue to his identity?
GEMELLUS:	Not much. The ancient writings are very general in nature.
HEROD:	Nothing to indicate his birthplace?
GEMELLUS:	There's one which relates to Bethlehem.
GAIUS:	Bethlehem?

GEMELLUS:	Bethlehem is the ancient city of King David. The passage runs something like this:
	And you, O Bethlehem,
	    who are little among the towns of Judah,
	From you shall come one
	    who is to be ruler in Israel.

HEROD:	It doesn't **say** that's his birth place.
GEMELLUS:	No. It's a poetic way of saying that someone of the lineage or spirit of David will come to the throne.

GAIUS:	No wonder these people are so unruly.
GEMELLUS:	But not all would support an insurrection. Some are more interested in religious or moral renewal. They believe God will send the king when the nation achieves true righteousness.
GAIUS:	*(laughing)* That may take some time.
NICOLAUS:	Others believe the coming king will be some superhuman, angelic being from heaven.
GEMELLUS:	Or the direct intervention of their God.
GAIUS:	*(jokingly)* That's tough competition!
HEROD:	*(butting in)* Let them dream their dreams. I'm more concerned with the here and now. In the tinder box of the present some group may use a young child as a rallying point.
GAIUS:	We don't have much to go on.
HEROD:	Only these Wise Men. *(He reflects for a moment.)* I'll call them back, give them this bit of information about Bethlehem and ask them to return when they locate the child. Festus! Bring back the Wise Men. *(Festus leaves.)*
NICOLAUS:	But will they return? Wouldn't it be better to torture the information out of them while we have them?
HEROD:	I don't think they know any more.
GAIUS:	By the time they find the child they may learn that you wouldn't be too favorably disposed to another prince.
HEROD:	That's a risk we'll have to take. They may be naive enough to return.
FESTUS:	The Wise Men, sir.
HEROD:	Come in, gentlemen. Please meet Nicolaus and Gemellus, my advisors. *(They stand and there are bows.)* We have discussed the matter of the young prince. It seems that many Jewish people trace their ancestry back to King David so the new prince might be anyone of that lineage. The only information which might help is a passage from one of their sacred books which refers to Bethlehem, a small village about five miles south of here.
GEMELLUS:	The ancient city of King David.
HEROD:	In view of my advancing years I am most interested in the matter. If this is the birth of the long promised Messiah, perhaps I could ensure that his claim to the throne receives our closest attention. When you have found him, bring me word that I may come and pay my respects.
MELCHIOR:	Thank you for this help. We will continue the search in eager expectation that this birth is of great significance.
HEROD:	I assure you it is of very great significance. We will wait to hear from you. *(The Wise Men leave.)*
GAIUS:	I hope we've been wise letting them go.
HEROD:	Don't worry. I have a contingency plan. The slaughter of all the young children in Bethlehem would certainly discourage any would-be aspirant.

GEMELLUS: *(with a pained, **not** defiant tone)* Good god. Not more bloodshed. Surely we've had enough.

HEROD: That's all some people understand.

GEMELLUS: But there's no proven danger. At worst your sons will quarrel over the succession and Rome will decide. There's no need to slaughter innocent children.

HEROD: If insurrection breaks out Rome will take direct control.

GEMELLUS: Put some of the rebels to death. But not the children.

HEROD: I can't take chances.

GEMELLUS: But we don't know there's a plot. Those Wise Men may be lunatic dreamers.

HEROD: I've learned not to trust anyone.

GEMELLUS: And look at what it's done. Your favorite wife and two sons killed. Your uncle gone.

HEROD: *(in another demented outburst)* But I'm still here! I've survived! I'm still king!

GEMELLUS: But at great cost. Your rule now rests on fear.

HEROD: Any other basis would be futile. Give some of these rebels an inch and they'd take a mile.

GEMELLUS: Surely one can be strong without being brutal. One needn't butcher innocent children. How will people feel about such slaughter?

HEROD: I've long since learned to ignore public sentiment.

GEMELLUS: You have no desire to be loved by your people?

HEROD: No.

GEMELLUS: Respected?

HEROD: They respect power.

GEMELLUS: None to mourn your passing?

HEROD: *(with insidious glee)* I can think of ways to make people mourn my death.

GEMELLUS: You can?

HEROD: Yes. Arrange to have the leading citizens put to death when I die. That will make the tears flow.

GEMELLUS: You must be mad to think such things. Your name will live in infamy.

HEROD: My name will live on as one who held power against great odds.

GEMELLUS: There are moments I think we must all be insane. There must be some better way.

HEROD: The way of those naive Wise Men? Wandering about on some crazy star led quest? Don't be a fool, Gemellus. What are a few more deaths? A hundred years from now no one will remember. The young prince, whoever he is, will be forgotten. The dreams of those Wise Men will still be wild dreams. Men will continue to survive by force as they always have.

GEMELLUS: I'm not trying to be foolish. One must use power to maintain order. But **brute** force staggers from one confrontation to the next.

HEROD: I wouldn't be too hopeful, Gemellus. As long as human nature remains what it is, people will scheme and fight and kill.

GEMELLUS: Unless they learn to struggle for peace and good will. Maybe this is what those old prophets had in mind when they spoke of a coming prince of peace . . . someone not interested in wealth, in fame, in a throne . . . someone only obscure Wise Men will be able to find.

HEROD: *(growing irritated)* Don't try my patience, Gemellus. I've put men to death for less insolence than that. You've been a good friend. I wouldn't want to lose you now. You're not going to change an old man. History will judge me as I am. *(struggling to his feet)* But enough talk for one day. I'm tired. Good night, gentlemen. *(He leaves and the lights, if any, fade. A voice is heard.)*

VOICE: Lo, the star which they had seen in the East went before them, till it came to rest over the place where the child was. When they saw the star, they rejoiced exceedingly with great joy; and going into the house they saw the child with Mary his mother, and they fell down and worshiped him. Then, opening their treasures, they offered him gifts, gold and frankincense and myrrh. . . . And being warned in a dream not to return to Herod, they departed to their own country by another way.

A Star Led Quest

TIME: Approximately 4 B.C.

PLACE: Herod's Throne Room

CHARACTERS: Festus: Herod's attendant
                Herod
                Gaius: an officer in charge of investigating subversion
                Melchior
                Balthazar
                Caspar
                Nicolaus: an advisor, harsh
                Gemellus: an advisor, somewhat mellow

FESTUS: *(entering)* Your Majesty, Gaius has arrived.

HEROD: Show him in.

GAIUS: You sent for me, sir?

HEROD: Yes. Sit down. *(a pause)* Some wine?

GAIUS: Please.

HEROD: Festus, some wine for the captain. *(Festus pours out a glass from a container and retires.)* Gaius, I want to discuss the behavior of Antipater. You may remember he's my eldest son by my first wife, Doris.

GAIUS: And logically, your successor.

HEROD: Perhaps. Although my sons Alexander and Aristobulus by my second wife Marianne always considered him a commoner.

GAIUS: But they were executed two years ago.

HEROD: Yes! For plotting treason! But that isn't why I called you, Gaius. I've heard that Antipater was involved in the death of my brother, Pheroras.

GAIUS: The poisoning?

HEROD: That I understand. What concerns me is the possibility he is maneuvering against me.

GAIUS: Why would he do that?

HEROD: With me so near death?

GAIUS: No, your majesty. I meant with Alexander and Aristobulus out of the way.

HEROD: Ah, captain, you forget that I have several other sons who might want the throne. Archelaus and Antipas by Malthace and Philip by Cleopatra.

GAIUS: But they are much younger than Antipater.

HEROD: That means little. Many people consider me a usurper. *(At this point Herod changes tone and bursts out with emotional rage.)* Usurper! I've saved the nation! Restored the economy! Rebuilt the Temple! Solomon did no more! Yet they call me a usurper! *(then in a more subdued tone)* My sons are bred with the same spirit. They wouldn't hesitate to eliminate me, much less a half-brother. I want you to investigate Antipater. If he has been engaged in plots against me, let me know.

FESTUS: *(re-entering)* Your majesty?

HEROD: What is it?

FESTUS: Three men have arrived at the court. They claim to be Wise Men from the East.

HEROD: Do they appear to be men of importance?

FESTUS: No, sir.

HEROD: Then send them on their way.

FESTUS: They seek information about a newborn king.

HEROD: *(struggling to his feet)* A what?

FESTUS: A king. A king of the Jews.

HEROD: Good god! Another claimant to the throne! That's all we need. *(He pauses a moment in deep thought.)* Bring them in at once. *(He painfully seats himself.)*

GAIUS: They might provide some useful information.

HEROD: Yes. Yes. But we must be careful. If we seem disturbed they might become suspicious. We may have stumbled upon another plot.

FESTUS: *(leading in the three Wise Men)* Your majesty, Melchior . . . Balthazar . . . Caspar. *(They bow as their names are called.)* Gentlemen, his majesty, Herod, king of Judea by order of Augustus Caesar, Emperor of Rome.

HEROD: Welcome, sirs. This is Captain Gaius, my attendant. *(Gaius bows to them and they bow in turn.)* I understand you come in search of a newborn king?

MELCHIOR: Yes. It is our understanding that a birth of great significance has taken place and we came to pay our respects to the newborn prince.

HEROD: And who gave you news of this birth?

BALTHAZAR: A star.

GAIUS: A star?

HEROD: Don't be surprised, Captain. You are now in the East where star gazing is an honorable profession. *(turning back to the Wise Men)* And what direction did the star provide?

CASPAR: It led us to Judea. When we reached Jerusalem we naturally thought people would be aware of the birth.

HEROD: Indeed you would. I must offer an explanation for my inability to give you an answer. As you can see I am an old man with little time to live. I had ten wives and many children. My progeny are numerous. Strange as it may seem I am unaware of any expected birth in this large family.

CASPAR: Has there been a birth in, say, the last two years?

HEROD: Why do you ask that?

BALTHAZAR: Because we have been studying the star for that period of time. The prince may be a year or two old by now.

HEROD: I see. And you have no other information? No name or place of birth?

MELCHIOR: None, sir.

HEROD: Gentlemen, I'm as much interested in locating this prince as you are. Perhaps some of my advisors might be able to help. If you'll retire for a few minutes I'll consult them. Festus!

FESTUS: Sir.

HEROD: Show these gentlemen to my private chambers and attend to their wants. And send Nicolaus and Gemellus to me at once. *(They leave and Herod turns to Gaius.)* We may be on to something important.

GAIUS: Could there be a Jewish claimant to the throne?

HEROD: Quite possibly. Many of the more nationalistic Jews have refused to recognize my right to the throne.

GAIUS: But what threat can a child pose?

HEROD: It's not the child. It's those who would use a child to promote rebellion.

FESTUS: Nicolaus and Gemellus, your majesty.

HEROD: Gentlemen.

NICOLAUS: You called.

HEROD: Yes. Come in and sit down. A few moments ago Gaius and I listened to a group of Wise Men from the East. They claimed they had been led by a star to seek a newborn king of the Jews. But they had no information about his identity or place of birth.

NICOLAUS: *(musing)* King of the Jews? They may have inadvertently picked up part of another plot.

HEROD: We've discussed that possibility. I'm sure some are hoping for a Jewish king on my death. Perhaps even before. But I know of no particular family which is making claim to royal privilege.

GEMELLUS: Many Jewish people trace their ancestry back to the Davidic kings.

NICOLAUS: And many expect a restoration of the Davidic dynasty.

HEROD: But would these expectations give a clue to his identity?

GEMELLUS: Not much. The ancient writings are very general in nature.

HEROD: Nothing to indicate his birthplace?

GEMELLUS: There's one which relates to Bethlehem.

GAIUS: Bethlehem?

GEMELLUS: Bethlehem is the ancient city of King David. The passage runs something like this:
> And you, O Bethlehem,
>   who are little among the towns of Judah,
> From you shall come one
>   who is to be ruler in Israel.

HEROD: It doesn't **say** that's his birth place.

GEMELLUS: No. It's a poetic way of saying that someone of the lineage or spirit of David will come to the throne.

GAIUS: No wonder these people are so unruly.

GEMELLUS: But not all would support an insurrection. Some are more interested in religious or moral renewal. They believe God will send the king when the nation achieves true righteousness.

GAIUS: *(laughing)* That may take some time.

NICOLAUS: Others believe the coming king will be some superhuman, angelic being from heaven.

GEMELLUS: Or the direct intervention of their God.

GAIUS: *(jokingly)* That's tough competition!

HEROD: *(butting in)* Let them dream their dreams. I'm more concerned with the here and now. In the tinder box of the present some group may use a young child as a rallying point.

GAIUS: We don't have much to go on.

HEROD: Only these Wise Men. *(He reflects for a moment.)* I'll call them back, give them this bit of information about Bethlehem and ask them to return when they locate the child. Festus! Bring back the Wise Men. *(Festus leaves.)*

NICOLAUS: But will they return? Wouldn't it be better to torture the information out of them while we have them?

HEROD: I don't think they know any more.

GAIUS: By the time they find the child they may learn that you wouldn't be too favorably disposed to another prince.

HEROD: That's a risk we'll have to take. They may be naive enough to return.

FESTUS: The Wise Men, sir.

HEROD: Come in, gentlemen. Please meet Nicolaus and Gemellus, my advisors. *(They stand and there are bows.)* We have discussed the matter of the young prince. It seems that many Jewish people trace their ancestry back to King David so the new prince might be anyone of that lineage. The only information which might help is a passage from one of their sacred books which refers to Bethlehem, a small village about five miles south of here.

GEMELLUS: The ancient city of King David.

HEROD: In view of my advancing years I am most interested in the matter. If this is the birth of the long promised Messiah, perhaps I could ensure that his claim to the throne receives our closest attention. When you have found him, bring me word that I may come and pay my respects.

MELCHIOR: Thank you for this help. We will continue the search in eager expectation that this birth is of great significance.

HEROD: I assure you it is of very great significance. We will wait to hear from you. *(The Wise Men leave.)*

GAIUS: I hope we've been wise letting them go.

HEROD: Don't worry. I have a contingency plan. The slaughter of all the young children in Bethlehem would certainly discourage any would-be aspirant.

GEMELLUS: *(with a pained, **not** defiant tone)* Good god. Not more bloodshed. Surely we've had enough.

HEROD: That's all some people understand.

GEMELLUS: But there's no proven danger. At worst your sons wi'l quarrel over the succession and Rome will decide. There's no need to slaughter innocent children.

HEROD: If insurrection breaks out Rome will take direct control.

GEMELLUS: Put some of the rebels to death. But not the children.

HEROD: I can't take chances.

GEMELLUS: But we don't know there's a plot. Those Wise Men may be lunatic dreamers.

HEROD: I've learned not to trust anyone.

GEMELLUS: And look at what it's done. Your favorite wife and two sons killed. Your uncle gone.

HEROD: *(in another demented outburst)* But I'm still here! I've survived! I'm still king!

GEMELLUS: But at great cost. Your rule now rests on fear.

HEROD: Any other basis would be futile. Give some of these rebels an inch and they'd take a mile.

GEMELLUS: Surely one can be strong without being brutal. One needn't butcher innocent children. How will people feel about such slaughter?

HEROD: I've long since learned to ignore public sentiment.

GEMELLUS: You have no desire to be loved by your people?

HEROD: No.

GEMELLUS: Respected?

HEROD: They respect power.

GEMELLUS: None to mourn your passing?

HEROD: *(with insidious glee)* I can think of ways to make people mourn my death.

GEMELLUS: You can?

HEROD: Yes. Arrange to have the leading citizens put to death when I die. That will make the tears flow.

GEMELLUS: You must be mad to think such things. Your name will live in infamy.

HEROD: My name will live on as one who held power against great odds.

GEMELLUS: There are moments I think we must all be insane. There must be some better way.

HEROD: The way of those naive Wise Men? Wandering about on some crazy star led quest? Don't be a fool, Gemellus. What are a few more deaths? A hundred years from now no one will remember. The young prince, whoever he is, will be forgotten. The dreams of those Wise Men will still be wild dreams. Men will continue to survive by force as they always have.

GEMELLUS: I'm not trying to be foolish. One must use power to maintain order. But **brute** force staggers from one confrontation to the next.

HEROD: I wouldn't be too hopeful, Gemellus. As long as human nature remains what it is, people will scheme and fight and kill.

GEMELLUS: Unless they learn to struggle for peace and good will. Maybe this is what those old prophets had in mind when they spoke of a coming prince of peace . . . someone not interested in wealth, in fame, in a throne . . . someone only obscure Wise Men will be able to find.

HEROD: *(growing irritated)* Don't try my patience, Gemellus. I've put men to death for less insolence than that. You've been a good friend. I wouldn't want to lose you now. You're not going to change an old man. History will judge me as I am. *(struggling to his feet)* But enough talk for one day. I'm tired. Good night, gentlemen. *(He leaves and the lights, if any, fade. A voice is heard.)*

VOICE: Lo, the star which they had seen in the East went before them, till it came to rest over the place where the child was. When they saw the star, they rejoiced exceedingly with great joy; and going into the house they saw the child with Mary his mother, and they fell down and worshiped him. Then, opening their treasures, they offered him gifts, gold and frankincense and myrrh. . . . And being warned in a dream not to return to Herod, they departed to their own country by another way.

A Star Led Quest

TIME: Approximately 4 B.C.

PLACE: Herod's Throne Room

CHARACTERS: Festus: Herod's attendant
               Herod
               Gaius: an officer in charge of investigating subversion
               Melchior
               Balthazar
               Caspar
               Nicolaus: an advisor, harsh
               Gemellus: an advisor, somewhat mellow

FESTUS: *(entering)* Your Majesty, Gaius has arrived.

HEROD: Show him in.

GAIUS: You sent for me, sir?

HEROD: Yes. Sit down. *(a pause)* Some wine?

GAIUS: Please.

HEROD: Festus, some wine for the captain. *(Festus pours out a glass from a container and retires.)* Gaius, I want to discuss the behavior of Antipater. You may remember he's my eldest son by my first wife, Doris.

GAIUS: And logically, your successor.

HEROD: Perhaps. Although my sons Alexander and Aristobulus by my second wife Marianne always considered him a commoner.

GAIUS: But they were executed two years ago.

HEROD: Yes! For plotting treason! But that isn't why I called you, Gaius. I've heard that Antipater was involved in the death of my brother, Pheroras.

GAIUS: The poisoning?

HEROD: That I understand. What concerns me is the possibility he is maneuvering against me.

GAIUS: Why would he do that?

HEROD: With me so near death?

GAIUS: No, your majesty. I meant with Alexander and Aristobulus out of the way.

HEROD: Ah, captain, you forget that I have several other sons who might want the throne. Archelaus and Antipas by Malthace and Philip by Cleopatra.

GAIUS: But they are much younger than Antipater.

HEROD: That means little. Many people consider me a usurper. *(At this point Herod changes tone and bursts out with emotional rage.)* Usurper! I've saved the nation! Restored the economy! Rebuilt the Temple! Solomon did no more! Yet they call me a usurper! *(then in a more subdued tone)* My sons are bred with the same spirit. They wouldn't hesitate to eliminate me, much less a half-brother. I want you to investigate Antipater. If he has been engaged in plots against me, let me know.

FESTUS: *(re-entering)* Your majesty?

HEROD: What is it?

FESTUS: Three men have arrived at the court. They claim to be Wise Men from the East.

HEROD: Do they appear to be men of importance?

FESTUS: No, sir.

HEROD: Then send them on their way.

FESTUS: They seek information about a newborn king.

HEROD: *(struggling to his feet)* A what?

FESTUS: A king. A king of the Jews.

HEROD: Good god! Another claimant to the throne! That's all we need. *(He pauses a moment in deep thought.)* Bring them in at once. *(He painfully seats himself.)*

GAIUS: They might provide some useful information.

HEROD: Yes. Yes. But we must be careful. If we seem disturbed they might become suspicious. We may have stumbled upon another plot.

FESTUS: *(leading in the three Wise Men)* Your majesty, Melchior . . . Balthazar . . . Caspar. *(They bow as their names are called.)* Gentlemen, his majesty, Herod, king of Judea by order of Augustus Caesar, Emperor of Rome.

HEROD: Welcome, sirs. This is Captain Gaius, my attendant. *(Gaius bows to them and they bow in turn.)* I understand you come in search of a newborn king?

MELCHIOR: Yes. It is our understanding that a birth of great significance has taken place and we came to pay our respects to the newborn prince.

HEROD: And who gave you news of this birth?

BALTHAZAR: A star.

GAIUS: A star?

HEROD: Don't be surprised, Captain. You are now in the East where star gazing is an honorable profession. *(turning back to the Wise Men)* And what direction did the star provide?

CASPAR: It led us to Judea. When we reached Jerusalem we naturally thought people would be aware of the birth.

HEROD: Indeed you would. I must offer an explanation for my inability to give you an answer. As you can see I am an old man with little time to live. I had ten wives and many children. My progeny are numerous. Strange as it may seem I am unaware of any expected birth in this large family.

CASPAR: Has there been a birth in, say, the last two years?

HEROD: Why do you ask that?

BALTHAZAR: Because we have been studying the star for that period of time. The prince may be a year or two old by now.

HEROD: I see. And you have no other information? No name or place of birth?

MELCHIOR: None, sir.

HEROD: Gentlemen, I'm as much interested in locating this prince as you are. Perhaps some of my advisors might be able to help. If you'll retire for a few minutes I'll consult them. Festus!

FESTUS: Sir.

HEROD: Show these gentlemen to my private chambers and attend to their wants. And send Nicolaus and Gemellus to me at once. *(They leave and Herod turns to Gaius.)* We may be on to something important.

GAIUS: Could there be a Jewish claimant to the throne?

HEROD: Quite possibly. Many of the more nationalistic Jews have refused to recognize my right to the throne.

GAIUS: But what threat can a child pose?

HEROD: It's not the child. It's those who would use a child to promote rebellion.

FESTUS: Nicolaus and Gemellus, your majesty.

HEROD: Gentlemen.

NICOLAUS: You called.

HEROD: Yes. Come in and sit down. A few moments ago Gaius and I listened to a group of Wise Men from the East. They claimed they had been led by a star to seek a newborn king of the Jews. But they had no information about his identity or place of birth.

NICOLAUS: *(musing)* King of the Jews? They may have inadvertently picked up part of another plot.

HEROD: We've discussed that possibility. I'm sure some are hoping for a Jewish king on my death. Perhaps even before. But I know of no particular family which is making claim to royal privilege.

GEMELLUS: Many Jewish people trace their ancestry back to the Davidic kings.

NICOLAUS: And many expect a restoration of the Davidic dynasty.

HEROD: But would these expectations give a clue to his identity?

GEMELLUS: Not much. The ancient writings are very general in nature.

HEROD: Nothing to indicate his birthplace?

GEMELLUS: There's one which relates to Bethlehem.

GAIUS: Bethlehem?

GEMELLUS: Bethlehem is the ancient city of King David. The passage runs something like this:
> And you, O Bethlehem,
>   who are little among the towns of Judah,
> From you shall come one
>   who is to be ruler in Israel.

HEROD: It doesn't **say** that's his birth place.

GEMELLUS: No. It's a poetic way of saying that someone of the lineage or spirit of David will come to the throne.

GAIUS: No wonder these people are so unruly.

GEMELLUS: But not all would support an insurrection. Some are more interested in religious or moral renewal. They believe God will send the king when the nation achieves true righteousness.

GAIUS: *(laughing)* That may take some time.

NICOLAUS: Others believe the coming king will be some superhuman, angelic being from heaven.

GEMELLUS: Or the direct intervention of their God.

GAIUS: *(jokingly)* That's tough competition!

HEROD: *(butting in)* Let them dream their dreams. I'm more concerned with the here and now. In the tinder box of the present some group may use a young child as a rallying point.

GAIUS: We don't have much to go on.

HEROD: Only these Wise Men. *(He reflects for a moment.)* I'll call them back, give them this bit of information about Bethlehem and ask them to return when they locate the child. Festus! Bring back the Wise Men. *(Festus leaves.)*

NICOLAUS: But will they return? Wouldn't it be better to torture the information out of them while we have them?

HEROD: I don't think they know any more.

GAIUS: By the time they find the child they may learn that you wouldn't be too favorably disposed to another prince.

HEROD: That's a risk we'll have to take. They may be naive enough to return.

FESTUS: The Wise Men, sir.

HEROD: Come in, gentlemen. Please meet Nicolaus and Gemellus, my advisors. *(They stand and there are bows.)* We have discussed the matter of the young prince. It seems that many Jewish people trace their ancestry back to King David so the new prince might be anyone of that lineage. The only information which might help is a passage from one of their sacred books which refers to Bethlehem, a small village about five miles south of here.

GEMELLUS: The ancient city of King David.

HEROD: In view of my advancing years I am most interested in the matter. If this is the birth of the long promised Messiah, perhaps I could ensure that his claim to the throne receives our closest attention. When you have found him, bring me word that I may come and pay my respects.

MELCHIOR: Thank you for this help. We will continue the search in eager expectation that this birth is of great significance.

HEROD: I assure you it is of very great significance. We will wait to hear from you. *(The Wise Men leave.)*

GAIUS: I hope we've been wise letting them go.

HEROD: Don't worry. I have a contingency plan. The slaughter of all the young children in Bethlehem would certainly discourage any would-be aspirant.

GEMELLUS: *(with a pained,* **not** *defiant tone)* Good god. Not more bloodshed. Surely we've had enough.

HEROD: That's all some people understand.

GEMELLUS: But there's no proven danger. At worst your sons will quarrel over the succession and Rome will decide. There's no need to slaughter innocent children.

HEROD: If insurrection breaks out Rome will take direct control.

GEMELLUS: Put some of the rebels to death. But not the children.

HEROD: I can't take chances.

GEMELLUS: But we don't know there's a plot. Those Wise Men may be lunatic dreamers.

HEROD: I've learned not to trust anyone.

GEMELLUS: And look at what it's done. Your favorite wife and two sons killed. Your uncle gone.

HEROD: *(in another demented outburst)* But I'm still here! I've survived! I'm still king!

GEMELLUS: But at great cost. Your rule now rests on fear.

HEROD: Any other basis would be futile. Give some of these rebels an inch and they'd take a mile.

GEMELLUS: Surely one can be strong without being brutal. One needn't butcher innocent children. How will people feel about such slaughter?

HEROD: I've long since learned to ignore public sentiment.

GEMELLUS: You have no desire to be loved by your people?

HEROD: No.

GEMELLUS: Respected?

HEROD: They respect power.

GEMELLUS: None to mourn your passing?

HEROD: *(with insidious glee)* I can think of ways to make people mourn my death.

GEMELLUS: You can?

HEROD: Yes. Arrange to have the leading citizens put to death when I die. That will make the tears flow.

GEMELLUS: You must be mad to think such things. Your name will live in infamy.

HEROD: My name will live on as one who held power against great odds.

GEMELLUS: There are moments I think we must all be insane. There must be some better way.

HEROD: The way of those naive Wise Men? Wandering about on some crazy star led quest? Don't be a fool, Gemellus. What are a few more deaths? A hundred years from now no one will remember. The young prince, whoever he is, will be forgotten. The dreams of those Wise Men will still be wild dreams. Men will continue to survive by force as they always have.

GEMELLUS: I'm not trying to be foolish. One must use power to maintain order. But **brute** force staggers from one confrontation to the next.

HEROD: I wouldn't be too hopeful, Gemellus. As long as human nature remains what it is, people will scheme and fight and kill.

GEMELLUS: Unless they learn to struggle for peace and good will. Maybe this is what those old prophets had in mind when they spoke of a coming prince of peace . . . someone not interested in wealth, in fame, in a throne . . . someone only obscure Wise Men will be able to find.

HEROD: *(growing irritated)* Don't try my patience, Gemellus. I've put men to death for less insolence than that. You've been a good friend. I wouldn't want to lose you now. You're not going to change an old man. History will judge me as I am. *(struggling to his feet)* But enough talk for one day. I'm tired. Good night, gentlemen. *(He leaves and the lights, if any, fade. A voice is heard.)*

VOICE: Lo, the star which they had seen in the East went before them, till it came to rest over the place where the child was. When they saw the star, they rejoiced exceedingly with great joy; and going into the house they saw the child with Mary his mother, and they fell down and worshiped him. Then, opening their treasures, they offered him gifts, gold and frankincense and myrrh. . . . And being warned in a dream not to return to Herod, they departed to their own country by another way.

A Star Led Quest

TIME: Approximately 4 B.C.

PLACE: Herod's Throne Room

CHARACTERS: Festus: Herod's attendant
Herod
Gaius: an officer in charge of investigating subversion
Melchior
Balthazar
Caspar
Nicolaus: an advisor, harsh
Gemellus: an advisor, somewhat mellow

FESTUS: *(entering)* Your Majesty, Gaius has arrived.

HEROD: Show him in.

GAIUS: You sent for me, sir?

HEROD: Yes. Sit down. *(a pause)* Some wine?

GAIUS: Please.

HEROD: Festus, some wine for the captain. *(Festus pours out a glass from a container and retires.)* Gaius, I want to discuss the behavior of Antipater. You may remember he's my eldest son by my first wife, Doris.

GAIUS: And logically, your successor.

HEROD: Perhaps. Although my sons Alexander and Aristobulus by my second wife Marianne always considered him a commoner.

GAIUS: But they were executed two years ago.

HEROD: Yes! For plotting treason! But that isn't why I called you, Gaius. I've heard that Antipater was involved in the death of my brother, Pheroras.

GAIUS: The poisoning?

HEROD: That I understand. What concerns me is the possibility he is maneuvering against me.

GAIUS: Why would he do that?

HEROD: With me so near death?

GAIUS: No, your majesty. I meant with Alexander and Aristobulus out of the way.

HEROD: Ah, captain, you forget that I have several other sons who might want the throne. Archelaus and Antipas by Malthace and Philip by Cleopatra.

GAIUS: But they are much younger than Antipater.

HEROD: That means little. Many people consider me a usurper. *(At this point Herod changes tone and bursts out with emotional rage.)* Usurper! I've saved the nation! Restored the economy! Rebuilt the Temple! Solomon did no more! Yet they call me a usurper! *(then in a more subdued tone)* My sons are bred with the same spirit. They wouldn't hesitate to eliminate me, much less a half-brother. I want you to investigate Antipater. If he has been engaged in plots against me, let me know.

FESTUS: *(re-entering)* Your majesty?

HEROD: What is it?

FESTUS: Three men have arrived at the court. They claim to be Wise Men from the East.

HEROD: Do they appear to be men of importance?

FESTUS: No, sir.

HEROD: Then send them on their way.

FESTUS: They seek information about a newborn king.

HEROD: *(struggling to his feet)* A what?

FESTUS: A king. A king of the Jews.

HEROD: Good god! Another claimant to the throne! That's all we need. *(He pauses a moment in deep thought.)* Bring them in at once. *(He painfully seats himself.)*

GAIUS: They might provide some useful information.

HEROD: Yes. Yes. But we must be careful. If we seem disturbed they might become suspicious. We may have stumbled upon another plot.

FESTUS: *(leading in the three Wise Men)* Your majesty, Melchior . . . Balthazar . . . Caspar. *(They bow as their names are called.)* Gentlemen, his majesty, Herod, king of Judea by order of Augustus Caesar, Emperor of Rome.

HEROD: Welcome, sirs. This is Captain Gaius, my attendant. *(Gaius bows to them and they bow in turn.)* I understand you come in search of a newborn king?

MELCHIOR: Yes. It is our understanding that a birth of great significance has taken place and we came to pay our respects to the newborn prince.

HEROD: And who gave you news of this birth?

BALTHAZAR: A star.

GAIUS: A star?

HEROD: Don't be surprised, Captain. You are now in the East where star gazing is an honorable profession. *(turning back to the Wise Men)* And what direction did the star provide?

CASPAR: It led us to Judea. When we reached Jerusalem we naturally thought people would be aware of the birth.

HEROD: Indeed you would. I must offer an explanation for my inability to give you an answer. As you can see I am an old man with little time to live. I had ten wives and many children. My progeny are numerous. Strange as it may seem I am unaware of any expected birth in this large family.

CASPAR: Has there been a birth in, say, the last two years?

HEROD: Why do you ask that?

BALTHAZAR: Because we have been studying the star for that period of time. The prince may be a year or two old by now.

HEROD: I see. And you have no other information? No name or place of birth?

MELCHIOR: None, sir.

HEROD: Gentlemen, I'm as much interested in locating this prince as you are. Perhaps some of my advisors might be able to help. If you'll retire for a few minutes I'll consult them. Festus!

FESTUS: Sir.

HEROD: Show these gentlemen to my private chambers and attend to their wants. And send Nicolaus and Gemellus to me at once. *(They leave and Herod turns to Gaius.)* We may be on to something important.

GAIUS: Could there be a Jewish claimant to the throne?

HEROD: Quite possibly. Many of the more nationalistic Jews have refused to recognize my right to the throne.

GAIUS: But what threat can a child pose?

HEROD: It's not the child. It's those who would use a child to promote rebellion.

FESTUS: Nicolaus and Gemellus, your majesty.

HEROD: Gentlemen.

NICOLAUS: You called.

HEROD: Yes. Come in and sit down. A few moments ago Gaius and I listened to a group of Wise Men from the East. They claimed they had been led by a star to seek a newborn king of the Jews. But they had no information about his identity or place of birth.

NICOLAUS: *(musing)* King of the Jews? They may have inadvertently picked up part of another plot.

HEROD: We've discussed that possibility. I'm sure some are hoping for a Jewish king on my death. Perhaps even before. But I know of no particular family which is making claim to royal privilege.

GEMELLUS: Many Jewish people trace their ancestry back to the Davidic kings.

NICOLAUS: And many expect a restoration of the Davidic dynasty.

HEROD: But would these expectations give a clue to his identity?

GEMELLUS: Not much. The ancient writings are very general in nature.

HEROD: Nothing to indicate his birthplace?

GEMELLUS: There's one which relates to Bethlehem.

GAIUS: Bethlehem?

GEMELLUS: Bethlehem is the ancient city of King David. The passage runs something like this:
> And you, O Bethlehem,
>   who are little among the towns of Judah,
> From you shall come one
>   who is to be ruler in Israel.

HEROD: It doesn't **say** that's his birth place.

GEMELLUS: No. It's a poetic way of saying that someone of the lineage or spirit of David will come to the throne.

GAIUS: No wonder these people are so unruly.

GEMELLUS: But not all would support an insurrection. Some are more interested in religious or moral renewal. They believe God will send the king when the nation achieves true righteousness.

GAIUS: *(laughing)* That may take some time.

NICOLAUS: Others believe the coming king will be some superhuman, angelic being from heaven.

GEMELLUS: Or the direct intervention of their God.

GAIUS: *(jokingly)* That's tough competition!

HEROD: *(butting in)* Let them dream their dreams. I'm more concerned with the here and now. In the tinder box of the present some group may use a young child as a rallying point.

GAIUS: We don't have much to go on.

HEROD: Only these Wise Men. *(He reflects for a moment.)* I'll call them back, give them this bit of information about Bethlehem and ask them to return when they locate the child. Festus! Bring back the Wise Men. *(Festus leaves.)*

NICOLAUS: But will they return? Wouldn't it be better to torture the information out of them while we have them?

HEROD: I don't think they know any more.

GAIUS: By the time they find the child they may learn that you wouldn't be too favorably disposed to another prince.

HEROD: That's a risk we'll have to take. They may be naive enough to return.

FESTUS: The Wise Men, sir.

HEROD: Come in, gentlemen. Please meet Nicolaus and Gemellus, my advisors. *(They stand and there are bows.)* We have discussed the matter of the young prince. It seems that many Jewish people trace their ancestry back to King David so the new prince might be anyone of that lineage. The only information which might help is a passage from one of their sacred books which refers to Bethlehem, a small village about five miles south of here.

GEMELLUS: The ancient city of King David.

HEROD: In view of my advancing years I am most interested in the matter. If this **is** the birth of the long promised Messiah, perhaps I could ensure that his claim to the throne receives our closest attention. When you have found him, bring me word that I may come and pay my respects.

MELCHIOR: Thank you for this help. We will continue the search in eager expectation that this birth is of great significance.

HEROD: I assure you it **is** of very great significance. We will wait to hear from you. *(The Wise Men leave.)*

GAIUS: I hope we've been wise letting them go.

HEROD: Don't worry. I have a contingency plan. The slaughter of all the young children in Bethlehem would certainly discourage any would-be aspirant.

GEMELLUS: *(with a pained,* **not** *defiant tone)* Good god. Not more bloodshed. Surely we've had enough.

HEROD: That's all some people understand.

GEMELLUS: But there's no proven danger. At worst your sons will quarrel over the succession and Rome will decide. There's no need to slaughter innocent children.

HEROD: If insurrection breaks out Rome will take direct control.

GEMELLUS: Put some of the rebels to death. But not the children.

HEROD: I can't take chances.

GEMELLUS: But we don't know there's a plot. Those Wise Men may be lunatic dreamers.

HEROD: I've learned not to trust anyone.

GEMELLUS: And look at what it's done. Your favorite wife and two sons killed. Your uncle gone.

HEROD: *(in another demented outburst)* But I'm still here! I've survived! I'm still king!

GEMELLUS: But at great cost. Your rule now rests on fear.

HEROD: Any other basis would be futile. Give some of these rebels an inch and they'd take a mile.

GEMELLUS: Surely one can be strong without being brutal. One needn't butcher innocent children. How will people feel about such slaughter?

HEROD: I've long since learned to ignore public sentiment.

GEMELLUS: You have no desire to be loved by your people?

HEROD: No.

GEMELLUS: Respected?

HEROD: They respect power.

GEMELLUS: None to mourn your passing?

HEROD: *(with insidious glee)* I can think of ways to make people mourn my death.

GEMELLUS: You can?

HEROD: Yes. Arrange to have the leading citizens put to death when I die. That will make the tears flow.

GEMELLUS: You must be mad to think such things. Your name will live in infamy.

HEROD: My name will live on as one who held power against great odds.

GEMELLUS: There are moments I think we must all be insane. There must be some better way.

HEROD: The way of those naive Wise Men? Wandering about on some crazy star led quest? Don't be a fool, Gemellus. What are a few more deaths? A hundred years from now no one will remember. The young prince, whoever he is, will be forgotten. The dreams of those Wise Men will still be wild dreams. Men will continue to survive by force as they always have.

GEMELLUS: I'm not trying to be foolish. One must use power to maintain order. But **brute** force staggers from one confrontation to the next.

HEROD: I wouldn't be too hopeful, Gemellus. As long as human nature remains what it is, people will scheme and fight and kill.

GEMELLUS: Unless they learn to struggle for peace and good will. Maybe this is what those old prophets had in mind when they spoke of a coming prince of peace . . . someone not interested in wealth, in fame, in a throne . . . someone only obscure Wise Men will be able to find.

HEROD: *(growing irritated)* Don't try my patience, Gemellus. I've put men to death for less insolence than that. You've been a good friend. I wouldn't want to lose you now. You're not going to change an old man. History will judge me as I am. *(struggling to his feet)* But enough talk for one day. I'm tired. Good night, gentlemen. *(He leaves and the lights, if any, fade. A voice is heard.)*

VOICE: Lo, the star which they had seen in the East went before them, till it came to rest over the place where the child was. When they saw the star, they rejoiced exceedingly with great joy; and going into the house they saw the child with Mary his mother, and they fell down and worshiped him. Then, opening their treasures, they offered him gifts, gold and frankincense and myrrh. . . . And being warned in a dream not to return to Herod, they departed to their own country by another way.

Fulfilled This Day

TIME: A Sabbath day in first century Palestine

PLACE: A synagogue

CHARACTERS: The Leader of the synagogue
                       Jesus
                       First man: a member of the congregation
                       Second man: also a member

(Jesus and the two men sit near the front of the nave in the midst of other members of the congregation who may be unaware of what is to happen. Some preliminary announcement is made that the first part of the service will be different from the usual opening. The leader stands in the chancel facing the congregation.)

LEADER: Blessed are You, O Lord, our God, Who formed light and created darkness, Who makes peace and creates all things, Who in mercy gives light to the earth and to those who dwell thereon, and in goodness renews the creation every day. With abounding love have you loved us, our God. With great and exceeding pity have you pitied us. Put into our hearts to understand, to discern, to mark, to learn, to teach, to heed, to do, and to fulfill in love all the words of your Law!

PEOPLE: Hear, O Israel: The Lord our God is one Lord; and you shall love the Lord your God with all your heart, and with all your soul, and with all your might. And these words which I command you this day shall be upon your heart; and you shall teach them diligently to your children, and shall talk of them when you sit in your house, and when you walk by the way, and when you lie down, and when you rise. And you shall bind them as a sign upon your hand, and they shall be as frontlets between your eyes. And you shall write them on the doorposts of your house and on your gates. *[Deuteronomy 6:4-9]*

LEADER: True and firm, established and enduring, right and faithful, beloved and precious, desirable and pleasant, well-ordered and acceptable, good and beautiful is Your word unto us forever and ever, our King and God, Who lives and endures, Who is high and exalted, great and revered, Who brings low the haughty, and raises up the lowly, leads forth the prisoners, delivers the meek, helps the poor, and answers His people when they cry unto Him. *(He takes up a scroll, unwinds it, and continues.)* Now Moses was keeping the flock of his father-in-law, Jethro, the priest of Midian; and he led his flock to the west side of the wilderness, and came to Horeb, the mountain of God. And the angel of the Lord appeared to him in a flame of fire out of the midst of a bush; and he looked, and lo, the bush was burning, yet it was not consumed. And Moses said, "I will turn aside and see this great sight, why the bush is not burnt." When the Lord saw that he turned aside to see, God called to him out of the bush, "Moses, Moses!" And he said, "Here am I." Then he said, "Do not come near; put off your shoes from your feet, for the place on which you are standing is holy ground." And he said, "I am the God of your father, the God of Abraham, the God of Isaac, and the God of Jacob." And Moses hid his face, for he was afraid to look at God.

                Then the Lord said, "I have seen the affliction of my people who are in Egypt, and have heard their cry because of their taskmasters; I know their sufferings, and I have come down to deliver them out of the hand of the Egyptians, and to bring them up out of that land to a good and broad land, a land flowing with milk and honey." *[Exodus 3:1-8]*

(Jesus stands from his place in the congregation and walks to the chancel. He picks up a second scroll and reads.)

JESUS: The Spirit of the Lord is upon me
    because he has anointed me to preach good news to the poor.
He has sent me to proclaim release to the captives
    and recovering of sight to the blind,
to set at liberty those who are oppressed,
    to proclaim the acceptable year of the Lord.
                      [Luke 4:18, 19 from Isaiah 61:1, 2 and 58:6]
(He closes the scroll, and sits down in the center of the chancel facing the congregation.) Today this scripture has been fulfilled in your hearing.   *[Luke: 4:21]*

LEADER: A beautiful reading from the prophet. We all long for the coming of that great day.

JESUS: That day has arrived.

LEADER: Are you saying the Lord's anointed has arrived?

JESUS: I'm saying that God has anointed me to this ministry.

FIRST MAN: And when did this take place?

JESUS: Several weeks ago . . . at the river Jordan.

FIRST MAN: And who anointed you?

JESUS: The spirit of God.

FIRST MAN: That isn't what I meant. Who was the person who anointed you?

JESUS: It was during my baptism at the hands of John.

(Some people in the congregation, who have rehearsed earlier, turn to one another in conversation.)

FIRST MAN: But John is baptizing sinners.

JESUS: John is calling for a genuine return to righteousness.

FIRST MAN: And you were unrighteous?

JESUS: Should we not all seek true righteousness?

SECOND MAN: Are you a disciple of John?

JESUS: No. But I respect his work.

SECOND MAN: Is John the long promised Messiah?

JESUS: He doesn't claim to be.

SECOND MAN: Is he Elijah brought back to life?

JESUS: John is preparing the way for the arrival of God's kingdom.

SECOND MAN: Do **you** claim to be the Messiah?

JESUS: I claim God has anointed me to the ministry described by Isaiah.

LEADER: But that **is** the ministry of the Messiah.

JESUS: So be it then.

FIRST MAN: Arrogance! Sheer arrogance! We all know who you are. You're Joseph's son. You're one of us. Your mother and brother and sisters live nearby. How can you make such a claim? If you **are** the anointed of God, give us some proof.

JESUS: You want me to prove my ministry?

FIRST MAN: Yes! We've heard rumors of what you did in Capernaum. Show us and perhaps we'll believe.

JESUS: What kind of sign do you want?

SECOND MAN: Turn a stone to bread. Moses was able to draw water from the rock in Horeb. Surely you should be able to do as much.

JESUS: Man shall not live by bread alone, but by every word that comes from the mouth of God.

SECOND MAN: You're not interested in the material welfare of God's people.

JESUS: I didn't say that. But I refuse to gain the loyalty of people by a miraculous provision of material goods.

SECOND MAN: You separate our material and spiritual needs?

JESUS: Quite the reverse. I **refuse** to separate them by limiting myself to one or the other.

FIRST MAN: But a spectacular miracle could win you the following you need. With such power you might drive the Romans from the land. Who knows? You might gain power over the whole world?

JESUS: I don't want such power. You shall worship the Lord your God. And him only shall you serve.

FIRST MAN: You expect to succeed without some change in our political and economic systems?

JESUS: I didn't say that. I say lasting justice and peace cannot be achieved by power separated from personal integrity.

LEADER: But surely you must offer some sign. Without that how can we be sure you are one called of God? How can you be sure yourself? Give a sign!

JESUS: We are not to test the Lord our God. My ministry must be its own test. You want a sign? The blind recover their sight, the lame walk, the lepers are cleansed, the deaf hear, the dead are raised to life, the poor are hearing the good news. What more do you want?

SECOND MAN: But you're obviously human, like ourselves.

JESUS: Doesn't God work through human flesh?

FIRST MAN: (*with a sneer*) Ordinary people like you?

JESUS: No prophet is accepted in his own country.

FIRST MAN: What do you mean?

JESUS: The prophets of old were often rejected by those who knew them. Jeremiah was imprisoned. Amos was advised to leave town.

FIRST MAN: You're putting yourself in the category of Jeremiah and Amos?

JESUS: I'm saying their work was not always accepted.

LEADER: And you say **your** work is to comfort the sorrowful, encourage the meek, befriend the lonely, heal the blind and lame and deaf, raise the dead and preach God's good news to the poor?

JESUS: Yes.

LEADER: Quite an ambitious undertaking.

FIRST MAN: And soon the whole world will be transformed?

JESUS: I don't expect an easy path. The servant of God may be despised and rejected; a man of sorrows, and acquainted with grief.

SECOND MAN: You said earlier that you were baptized by John.

JESUS: Yes.

SECOND MAN: You obviously feel he is a man of God.

JESUS: Among those born of women none is greater than John.

SECOND MAN: And yet with such credentials John isn't the Messiah?

JESUS: John prepares the way for the coming of God's kingdom. He is a very humble man. He who is least in the kingdom of God is greater than John.

SECOND MAN: Do you share John's attitude to Gentile people?

JESUS: That they too can be received into God's kingdom?

SECOND MAN: That isn't what I meant. You know that Judaism makes provision for the reception of Gentiles.

JESUS: Through a very elaborate process of purification.

SECOND MAN: Correct. John seems to have rejected that procedure.

JESUS: He calls for repentance and a baptism representing God's cleansing.

LEADER: True. But John's baptism is different from our proselyte baptism.

JESUS: Because he calls us to baptism as well?

LEADER: Precisely. He destroys the difference.

JESUS: There is a difference?

FIRST MAN: Of course there's a difference. How can you deny the past history of your people?

JESUS: I'm not denying our past history. But are we any more righteous than other people?

SECOND MAN: We don't deny the need to repent. But proselyte baptism symbolizes the need for serious purification.

JESUS: And you don't think we have such need?

SECOND MAN: *(with annoyance)* Are you one of those strange Essenes who think we need to be baptized every day?

JESUS: I don't call for that.

SECOND MAN: I'm relieved. But you won't admit that John is a religious fanatic?

(There is noise in the congregation to indicate not all share this view of John.)

JESUS: If I were to say that, I'd have to reject many of the prophets.

FIRST MAN: But who before John has suggested that Jew and non-Jew stand equal before God?

JESUS: Have you heard of Elijah?

FIRST MAN: *(with annoyance)* Of course we have.

JESUS: Have you heard, "There were many widows in Israel in the days of Elijah, when the heaven was shut up three years and six months, when there came a great famine over all the land." [*Luke 4:25*]

FIRST MAN: Yes.

JESUS: To whom was Elijah sent?

FIRST MAN: To Zarephath.

JESUS: In the land of Sidon.

FIRST MAN: Yes.

JESUS: A Gentile. *(murmur in the congregation)* And have you heard of Elisha? *(silence)* There were many lepers in Israel in the time of the prophet Elisha. And who was cleansed? *(silence)* Who?

SECOND MAN: *(reluctantly)* Naaman.

JESUS: The Syrian. . . . Another Gentile.

LEADER: You mean to say you're going to reject your own people and minister to the Gentiles.

JESUS: Not at all. I'm Jewish and I'm called to minister to my own people. I don't intend to proselytize the Gentiles. But neither do I deny that the grace of God can be at work in their lives.

LEADER: That is very generous, young man. But it threatens the very foundation of our faith.

JESUS: I think not. It is a fulfillment of the deepest conviction of our faith. Joel promised that one day God would pour out his spirit upon all flesh.

FIRST MAN: He was speaking to our people.

JESUS: It is a light thing that you should be my servant to raise up the tribes of Jacob, and to restore the preserved of Israel. I will also give you for a light to the Gentiles, that you may be my salvation unto the end of the earth.

(Individuals in the congregation stand, one after another in a growing crescendo.)

Blasphemy!

Throw him out!

Such arrogance!

Kill him!

(The Leader hurries to stand between Jesus and the angry congregation, raising his arms to pacify them. When the noise has subsided, he turns about to Jesus.)

LEADER: I think perhaps you should leave.

JESUS: You're right. I have offended some. But blessed is the man who is not offended in me. I speak the truth in love and will force no one. Shalom! *(He slowly walks the length of the church and out.)*

Fulfilled This Day

TIME: A Sabbath day in first century Palestine

PLACE: A synagogue

CHARACTERS: The Leader of the synagogue
                  Jesus
                  First man: a member of the congregation
                  Second man: also a member

(Jesus and the two men sit near the front of the nave in the midst of other members of the congregation who may be unaware of what is to happen. Some preliminary announcement is made that the first part of the service will be different from the usual opening. The leader stands in the chancel facing the congregation.)

LEADER: Blessed are You, O Lord, our God, Who formed light and created darkness, Who makes peace and creates all things, Who in mercy gives light to the earth and to those who dwell thereon, and in goodness renews the creation every day. With abounding love have you loved us, our God. With great and exceeding pity have you pitied us. Put into our hearts to understand, to discern, to mark, to learn, to teach, to heed, to do, and to fulfill in love all the words of your Law!

PEOPLE: Hear, O Israel: The Lord our God is one Lord; and you shall love the Lord your God with all your heart, and with all your soul, and with all your might. And these words which I command you this day shall be upon your heart; and you shall teach them diligently to your children, and shall talk of them when you sit in your house, and when you walk by the way, and when you lie down, and when you rise. And you shall bind them as a sign upon your hand, and they shall be as frontlets between your eyes. And you shall write them on the doorposts of your house and on your gates. *[Deuteronomy 6:4-9]*

LEADER: True and firm, established and enduring, right and faithful, beloved and precious, desirable and pleasant, well-ordered and acceptable, good and beautiful is Your word unto us forever and ever, our King and God, Who lives and endures, Who is high and exalted, great and revered, Who brings low the haughty, and raises up the lowly, leads forth the prisoners, delivers the meek, helps the poor, and answers His people when they cry unto Him. *(He takes up a scroll, unwinds it, and continues.)* Now Moses was keeping the flock of his father-in-law, Jethro, the priest of Midian; and he led his flock to the west side of the wilderness, and came to Horeb, the mountain of God. And the angel of the Lord appeared to him in a flame of fire out of the midst of a bush; and he looked, and lo, the bush was burning, yet it was not consumed. And Moses said, "I will turn aside and see this great sight, why the bush is not burnt." When the Lord saw that he turned aside to see, God called to him out of the bush, "Moses, Moses!" And he said, "Here am I." Then he said, "Do not come near; put off your shoes from your feet, for the place on which you are standing is holy ground." And he said, "I am the God of your father, the God of Abraham, the God of Isaac, and the God of Jacob." And Moses hid his face, for he was afraid to look at God.

Then the Lord said, "I have seen the affliction of my people who are in Egypt, and have heard their cry because of their taskmasters; I know their sufferings, and I have come down to deliver them out of the hand of the Egyptians, and to bring them up out of that land to a good and broad land, a land flowing with milk and honey." *[Exodus 3:1-8]*

(Jesus stands from his place in the congregation and walks to the chancel. He picks up a second scroll and reads.)

JESUS: The Spirit of the Lord is upon me
    because he has anointed me to preach good news to the poor.
He has sent me to proclaim release to the captives
    and recovering of sight to the blind,
to set at liberty those who are oppressed,
    to proclaim the acceptable year of the Lord.
                  [Luke 4:18, 19 from Isaiah 61:1, 2 and 58:6]
(He closes the scroll, and sits down in the center of the chancel facing the congregation.) Today this scripture has been fulfilled in your hearing.   *[Luke: 4:21]*

LEADER: A beautiful reading from the prophet. We all long for the coming of that great day.

JESUS: That day has arrived.

LEADER: Are you saying the Lord's anointed has arrived?

JESUS: I'm saying that God has anointed me to this ministry.

FIRST MAN: And when did this take place?

JESUS: Several weeks ago . . . at the river Jordan.

FIRST MAN: And who anointed you?

JESUS: The spirit of God.

FIRST MAN: That isn't what I meant. Who was the person who anointed you?

JESUS: It was during my baptism at the hands of John.

(Some people in the congregation, who have rehearsed earlier, turn to one another in conversation.)

FIRST MAN: But John is baptizing sinners.

JESUS: John is calling for a genuine return to righteousness.

FIRST MAN: And you were unrighteous?

JESUS: Should we not all seek true righteousness?

SECOND MAN: Are you a disciple of John?

JESUS: No. But I respect his work.

SECOND MAN: Is John the long promised Messiah?

JESUS: He doesn't claim to be.

SECOND MAN: Is he Elijah brought back to life?

JESUS: John is preparing the way for the arrival of God's kingdom.

SECOND MAN: Do **you** claim to be the Messiah?

JESUS: I claim God has anointed me to the ministry described by Isaiah.

LEADER: But that **is** the ministry of the Messiah.

JESUS: So be it then.

FIRST MAN:	Arrogance! Sheer arrogance! We all know who you are. You're Joseph's son. You're one of us. Your mother and brother and sisters live nearby. How can you make such a claim? If you **are** the anointed of God, give us some proof.
JESUS:	You want me to prove my ministry?
FIRST MAN:	Yes! We've heard rumors of what you did in Capernaum. Show us and perhaps we'll believe.
JESUS:	What kind of sign do you want?
SECOND MAN:	Turn a stone to bread. Moses was able to draw water from the rock in Horeb. Surely you should be able to do as much.
JESUS:	Man shall not live by bread alone, but by every word that comes from the mouth of God.
SECOND MAN:	You're not interested in the material welfare of God's people.
JESUS:	I didn't say that. But I refuse to gain the loyalty of people by a miraculous provision of material goods.
SECOND MAN:	You separate our material and spiritual needs?
JESUS:	Quite the reverse. I **refuse** to separate them by limiting myself to one or the other.
FIRST MAN:	But a spectacular miracle could win you the following you need. With such power you might drive the Romans from the land. Who knows? You might gain power over the whole world?
JESUS:	I don't want such power. You shall worship the Lord your God. And him only shall you serve.
FIRST MAN:	You expect to succeed without some change in our political and economic systems?
JESUS:	I didn't say that. I say lasting justice and peace cannot be achieved by power separated from personal integrity.
LEADER:	But surely you must offer some sign. Without that how can we be sure you are one called of God? How can you be sure yourself? Give a sign!
JESUS:	We are not to test the Lord our God. My ministry must be its own test. You want a sign? The blind recover their sight, the lame walk, the lepers are cleansed, the deaf hear, the dead are raised to life, the poor are hearing the good news. What more do you want?
SECOND MAN:	But you're obviously human, like ourselves.
JESUS:	Doesn't God work through human flesh?
FIRST MAN:	*(with a sneer)* Ordinary people like you?
JESUS:	No prophet is accepted in his own country.
FIRST MAN:	What do you mean?
JESUS:	The prophets of old were often rejected by those who knew them. Jeremiah was imprisoned. Amos was advised to leave town.
FIRST MAN:	You're putting yourself in the category of Jeremiah and Amos?

JESUS:	I'm saying their work was not always accepted.
LEADER:	And you say **your** work is to comfort the sorrowful, encourage the meek, befriend the lonely, heal the blind and lame and deaf, raise the dead and preach God's good news to the poor?
JESUS:	Yes.
LEADER:	Quite an ambitious undertaking.
FIRST MAN:	And soon the whole world will be transformed?
JESUS:	I don't expect an easy path. The servant of God may be despised and rejected; a man of sorrows, and acquainted with grief.
SECOND MAN:	You said earlier that you were baptized by John.
JESUS:	Yes.
SECOND MAN:	You obviously feel he is a man of God.
JESUS:	Among those born of women none is greater than John.
SECOND MAN:	And yet with such credentials John isn't the Messiah?
JESUS:	John prepares the way for the coming of God's kingdom. He is a very humble man. He who is least in the kingdom of God is greater than John.
SECOND MAN:	Do you share John's attitude to Gentile people?
JESUS:	That they too can be received into God's kingdom?
SECOND MAN:	That isn't what I meant. You know that Judaism makes provision for the reception of Gentiles.
JESUS:	Through a very elaborate process of purification.
SECOND MAN:	Correct. John seems to have rejected that procedure.
JESUS:	He calls for repentance and a baptism representing God's cleansing.
LEADER:	True. But John's baptism is different from our proselyte baptism.
JESUS:	Because he calls us to baptism as well?
LEADER:	Precisely. He destroys the difference.
JESUS:	There is a difference?
FIRST MAN:	Of course there's a difference. How can you deny the past history of your people?
JESUS:	I'm not denying our past history. But are we any more righteous than other people?
SECOND MAN:	We don't deny the need to repent. But proselyte baptism symbolizes the need for serious purification.
JESUS:	And you don't think we have such need?
SECOND MAN:	*(with annoyance)* Are you one of those strange Essenes who think we need to be baptized every day?
JESUS:	I don't call for that.
SECOND MAN:	I'm relieved. But you won't admit that John is a religious fanatic?

(There is noise in the congregation to indicate not all share this view of John.)

JESUS: If I were to say that, I'd have to reject many of the prophets.

FIRST MAN: But who before John has suggested that Jew and non-Jew stand equal before God?

JESUS: Have you heard of Elijah?

FIRST MAN: *(with annoyance)* Of course we have.

JESUS: Have you heard, "There were many widows in Israel in the days of Elijah, when the heaven was shut up three years and six months, when there came a great famine over all the land." *[Luke 4:25]*

FIRST MAN: Yes.

JESUS: To whom was Elijah sent?

FIRST MAN: To Zarephath.

JESUS: In the land of Sidon.

FIRST MAN: Yes.

JESUS: A Gentile. *(murmur in the congregation)* And have you heard of Elisha? *(silence)* There were many lepers in Israel in the time of the prophet Elisha. And who was cleansed? *(silence)* Who?

SECOND MAN: *(reluctantly)* Naaman.

JESUS: The Syrian. . . . Another Gentile.

LEADER: You mean to say you're going to reject your own people and minister to the Gentiles.

JESUS: Not at all. I'm Jewish and I'm called to minister to my own people. I don't intend to proselytize the Gentiles. But neither do I deny that the grace of God can be at work in their lives.

LEADER: That is very generous, young man. But it threatens the very foundation of our faith.

JESUS: I think not. It is a fulfillment of the deepest conviction of our faith. Joel promised that one day God would pour out his spirit upon all flesh.

FIRST MAN: He was speaking to our people.

JESUS: It is a light thing that you should be my servant to raise up the tribes of Jacob, and to restore the preserved of Israel. I will also give you for a light to the Gentiles, that you may be my salvation unto the end of the earth.

(Individuals in the congregation stand, one after another in a growing crescendo.)

Blasphemy!

Throw him out!

Such arrogance!

Kill him!

(The Leader hurries to stand between Jesus and the angry congregation, raising his arms to pacify them. When the noise has subsided, he turns about to Jesus.)

LEADER: I think perhaps you should leave.

JESUS: You're right. I have offended some. But blessed is the man who is not offended in me. I speak the truth in love and will force no one. Shalom! *(He slowly walks the length of the church and out.)*

Fulfilled This Day

TIME: A Sabbath day in first century Palestine

PLACE: A synagogue

CHARACTERS: The Leader of the synagogue
                  Jesus
                  First man: a member of the congregation
                  Second man: also a member

(Jesus and the two men sit near the front of the nave in the midst of other members of the congregation who may be unaware of what is to happen. Some preliminary announcement is made that the first part of the service will be different from the usual opening. The leader stands in the chancel facing the congregation.)

LEADER: Blessed are You, O Lord, our God, Who formed light and created darkness, Who makes peace and creates all things, Who in mercy gives light to the earth and to those who dwell thereon, and in goodness renews the creation every day. With abounding love have you loved us, our God. With great and exceeding pity have you pitied us. Put into our hearts to understand, to discern, to mark, to learn, to teach, to heed, to do, and to fulfill in love all the words of your Law!

PEOPLE: Hear, O Israel: The Lord our God is one Lord; and you shall love the Lord your God with all your heart, and with all your soul, and with all your might. And these words which I command you this day shall be upon your heart; and you shall teach them diligently to your children, and shall talk of them when you sit in your house, and when you walk by the way, and when you lie down, and when you rise. And you shall bind them as a sign upon your hand, and they shall be as frontlets between your eyes. And you shall write them on the doorposts of your house and on your gates. *[Deuteronomy 6:4-9]*

LEADER: True and firm, established and enduring, right and faithful, beloved and precious, desirable and pleasant, well-ordered and acceptable, good and beautiful is Your word unto us forever and ever, our King and God, Who lives and endures, Who is high and exalted, great and revered, Who brings low the haughty, and raises up the lowly, leads forth the prisoners, delivers the meek, helps the poor, and answers His people when they cry unto Him. *(He takes up a scroll, unwinds it, and continues.)* Now Moses was keeping the flock of his father-in-law, Jethro, the priest of Midian; and he led his flock to the west side of the wilderness, and came to Horeb, the mountain of God. And the angel of the Lord appeared to him in a flame of fire out of the midst of a bush; and he looked, and lo, the bush was burning, yet it was not consumed. And Moses said, "I will turn aside and see this great sight, why the bush is not burnt." When the Lord saw that he turned aside to see, God called to him out of the bush, "Moses, Moses!" And he said, "Here am I." Then he said, "Do not come near; put off your shoes from your feet, for the place on which you are standing is holy ground." And he said, "I am the God of your father, the God of Abraham, the God of Isaac, and the God of Jacob." And Moses hid his face, for he was afraid to look at God.

                Then the Lord said, "I have seen the affliction of my people who are in Egypt, and have heard their cry because of their taskmasters; I know their sufferings, and I have come down to deliver them out of the hand of the Egyptians, and to bring them up out of that land to a good and broad land, a land flowing with milk and honey." *[Exodus 3:1-8]*

(Jesus stands from his place in the congregation and walks to the chancel. He picks up a second scroll and reads.)

JESUS: The Spirit of the Lord is upon me
    because he has anointed me to preach good news to the poor.
He has sent me to proclaim release to the captives
    and recovering of sight to the blind,
to set at liberty those who are oppressed,
    to proclaim the acceptable year of the Lord.
                    [Luke 4:18, 19 from Isaiah 61:1, 2 and 58:6]
(He closes the scroll, and sits down in the center of the chancel facing the congregation.) Today this scripture has been fulfilled in your hearing.   *[Luke: 4:21]*

LEADER: A beautiful reading from the prophet. We all long for the coming of that great day.

JESUS: That day has arrived.

LEADER: Are you saying the Lord's anointed has arrived?

JESUS: I'm saying that God has anointed me to this ministry.

FIRST MAN: And when did this take place?

JESUS: Several weeks ago . . . at the river Jordan.

FIRST MAN: And who anointed you?

JESUS: The spirit of God.

FIRST MAN: That isn't what I meant. Who was the person who anointed you?

JESUS: It was during my baptism at the hands of John.

(Some people in the congregation, who have rehearsed earlier, turn to one another in conversation.)

FIRST MAN: But John is baptizing sinners.

JESUS: John is calling for a genuine return to righteousness.

FIRST MAN: And you were unrighteous?

JESUS: Should we not all seek true righteousness?

SECOND MAN: Are you a disciple of John?

JESUS: No. But I respect his work.

SECOND MAN: Is John the long promised Messiah?

JESUS: He doesn't claim to be.

SECOND MAN: Is he Elijah brought back to life?

JESUS: John is preparing the way for the arrival of God's kingdom.

SECOND MAN: Do **you** claim to be the Messiah?

JESUS: I claim God has anointed me to the ministry described by Isaiah.

LEADER: But that **is** the ministry of the Messiah.

JESUS: So be it then.

FIRST MAN: Arrogance! Sheer arrogance! We all know who you are. You're Joseph's son. You're one of us. Your mother and brother and sisters live nearby. How can you make such a claim? If you **are** the anointed of God, give us some proof.

JESUS: You want me to prove my ministry?

FIRST MAN: Yes! We've heard rumors of what you did in Capernaum. Show us and perhaps we'll believe.

JESUS: What kind of sign do you want?

SECOND MAN: Turn a stone to bread. Moses was able to draw water from the rock in Horeb. Surely you should be able to do as much.

JESUS: Man shall not live by bread alone, but by every word that comes from the mouth of God.

SECOND MAN: You're not interested in the material welfare of God's people.

JESUS: I didn't say that. But I refuse to gain the loyalty of people by a miraculous provision of material goods.

SECOND MAN: You separate our material and spiritual needs?

JESUS: Quite the reverse. I **refuse** to separate them by limiting myself to one or the other.

FIRST MAN: But a spectacular miracle could win you the following you need. With such power you might drive the Romans from the land. Who knows? You might gain power over the whole world?

JESUS: I don't want such power. You shall worship the Lord your God. And him only shall you serve.

FIRST MAN: You expect to succeed without some change in our political and economic systems?

JESUS: I didn't say that. I say lasting justice and peace cannot be achieved by power separated from personal integrity.

LEADER: But surely you must offer some sign. Without that how can we be sure you are one called of God? How can you be sure yourself? Give a sign!

JESUS: We are not to test the Lord our God. My ministry must be its own test. You want a sign? The blind recover their sight, the lame walk, the lepers are cleansed, the deaf hear, the dead are raised to life, the poor are hearing the good news. What more do you want?

SECOND MAN: But you're obviously human, like ourselves.

JESUS: Doesn't God work through human flesh?

FIRST MAN: *(with a sneer)* Ordinary people like you?

JESUS: No prophet is accepted in his own country.

FIRST MAN: What do you mean?

JESUS: The prophets of old were often rejected by those who knew them. Jeremiah was imprisoned. Amos was advised to leave town.

FIRST MAN: You're putting yourself in the category of Jeremiah and Amos?

JESUS: I'm saying their work was not always accepted.

LEADER: And you say **your** work is to comfort the sorrowful, encourage the meek, befriend the lonely, heal the blind and lame and deaf, raise the dead and preach God's good news to the poor?

JESUS: Yes.

LEADER: Quite an ambitious undertaking.

FIRST MAN: And soon the whole world will be transformed?

JESUS: I don't expect an easy path. The servant of God may be despised and rejected; a man of sorrows, and acquainted with grief.

SECOND MAN: You said earlier that you were baptized by John.

JESUS: Yes.

SECOND MAN: You obviously feel he is a man of God.

JESUS: Among those born of women none is greater than John.

SECOND MAN: And yet with such credentials John isn't the Messiah?

JESUS: John prepares the way for the coming of God's kingdom. He is a very humble man. He who is least in the kingdom of God is greater than John.

SECOND MAN: Do you share John's attitude to Gentile people?

JESUS: That they too can be received into God's kingdom?

SECOND MAN: That isn't what I meant. You know that Judaism makes provision for the reception of Gentiles.

JESUS: Through a very elaborate process of purification.

SECOND MAN: Correct. John seems to have rejected that procedure.

JESUS: He calls for repentance and a baptism representing God's cleansing.

LEADER: True. But John's baptism is different from our proselyte baptism.

JESUS: Because he calls us to baptism as well?

LEADER: Precisely. He destroys the difference.

JESUS: There is a difference?

FIRST MAN: Of course there's a difference. How can you deny the past history of your people?

JESUS: I'm not denying our past history. But are we any more righteous than other people?

SECOND MAN: We don't deny the need to repent. But proselyte baptism symbolizes the need for serious purification.

JESUS: And you don't think we have such need?

SECOND MAN: *(with annoyance)* Are you one of those strange Essenes who think we need to be baptized every day?

JESUS: I don't call for that.

SECOND MAN: I'm relieved. But you won't admit that John is a religious fanatic?

(There is noise in the congregation to indicate not all share this view of John.)

JESUS: If I were to say that, I'd have to reject many of the prophets.

FIRST MAN: But who before John has suggested that Jew and non-Jew stand equal before God?

JESUS: Have you heard of Elijah?

FIRST MAN: *(with annoyance)* Of course we have.

JESUS: Have you heard, "There were many widows in Israel in the days of Elijah, when the heaven was shut up three years and six months, when there came a great famine over all the land."   [*Luke 4:25*]

FIRST MAN: Yes.

JESUS: To whom was Elijah sent?

FIRST MAN: To Zarephath.

JESUS: In the land of Sidon.

FIRST MAN: Yes.

JESUS: A Gentile. *(murmur in the congregation)* And have you heard of Elisha? *(silence)* There were many lepers in Israel in the time of the prophet Elisha. And who was cleansed? *(silence)* Who?

SECOND MAN: *(reluctantly)* Naaman.

JESUS: The Syrian. . . . Another Gentile.

LEADER: You mean to say you're going to reject your own people and minister to the Gentiles.

JESUS: Not at all. I'm Jewish and I'm called to minister to my own people. I don't intend to proselytize the Gentiles. But neither do I deny that the grace of God can be at work in their lives.

LEADER: That is very generous, young man. But it threatens the very foundation of our faith.

JESUS: I think not. It is a fulfillment of the deepest conviction of our faith. Joel promised that one day God would pour out his spirit upon all flesh.

FIRST MAN: He was speaking to our people.

JESUS: It is a light thing that you should be my servant to raise up the tribes of Jacob, and to restore the preserved of Israel. I will also give you for a light to the Gentiles, that you may be my salvation unto the end of the earth.

(Individuals in the congregation stand, one after another in a growing crescendo.)

Blasphemy!

Throw him out!

Such arrogance!

Kill him!

(The Leader hurries to stand between Jesus and the angry congregation, raising his arms to pacify them. When the noise has subsided, he turns about to Jesus.)

LEADER: I think perhaps you should leave.

JESUS: You're right. I have offended some. But blessed is the man who is not offended in me. I speak the truth in love and will force no one. Shalom! *(He slowly walks the length of the church and out.)*

Fulfilled This Day

TIME: A Sabbath day in first century Palestine

PLACE: A synagogue

CHARACTERS: The Leader of the synagogue
Jesus
First man: a member of the congregation
Second man: also a member

(Jesus and the two men sit near the front of the nave in the midst of other members of the congregation who may be unaware of what is to happen. Some preliminary announcement is made that the first part of the service will be different from the usual opening. The leader stands in the chancel facing the congregation.)

LEADER: Blessed are You, O Lord, our God, Who formed light and created darkness, Who makes peace and creates all things, Who in mercy gives light to the earth and to those who dwell thereon, and in goodness renews the creation every day. With abounding love have you loved us, our God. With great and exceeding pity have you pitied us. Put into our hearts to understand, to discern, to mark, to learn, to teach, to heed, to do, and to fulfill in love all the words of your Law!

PEOPLE: Hear, O Israel: The Lord our God is one Lord; and you shall love the Lord your God with all your heart, and with all your soul, and with all your might. And these words which I command you this day shall be upon your heart; and you shall teach them diligently to your children, and shall talk of them when you sit in your house, and when you walk by the way, and when you lie down, and when you rise. And you shall bind them as a sign upon your hand, and they shall be as frontlets between your eyes. And you shall write them on the doorposts of your house and on your gates. *[Deuteronomy 6:4-9]*

LEADER: True and firm, established and enduring, right and faithful, beloved and precious, desirable and pleasant, well-ordered and acceptable, good and beautiful is Your word unto us forever and ever, our King and God, Who lives and endures, Who is high and exalted, great and revered, Who brings low the haughty, and raises up the lowly, leads forth the prisoners, delivers the meek, helps the poor, and answers His people when they cry unto Him. *(He takes up a scroll, unwinds it, and continues.)* Now Moses was keeping the flock of his father-in-law, Jethro, the priest of Midian; and he led his flock to the west side of the wilderness, and came to Horeb, the mountain of God. And the angel of the Lord appeared to him in a flame of fire out of the midst of a bush; and he looked, and lo, the bush was burning, yet it was not consumed. And Moses said, "I will turn aside and see this great sight, why the bush is not burnt." When the Lord saw that he turned aside to see, God called to him out of the bush, "Moses, Moses!" And he said, "Here am I." Then he said, "Do not come near; put off your shoes from your feet, for the place on which you are standing is holy ground." And he said, "I am the God of your father, the God of Abraham, the God of Isaac, and the God of Jacob." And Moses hid his face, for he was afraid to look at God.

Then the Lord said, "I have seen the affliction of my people who are in Egypt, and have heard their cry because of their taskmasters; I know their sufferings, and I have come down to deliver them out of the hand of the Egyptians, and to bring them up out of that land to a good and broad land, a land flowing with milk and honey." *[Exodus 3:1-8]*

(Jesus stands from his place in the congregation and walks to the chancel. He picks up a second scroll and reads.)

JESUS: The Spirit of the Lord is upon me
    because he has anointed me to preach good news to the poor.
He has sent me to proclaim release to the captives
    and recovering of sight to the blind,
to set at liberty those who are oppressed,
    to proclaim the acceptable year of the Lord.

                    [Luke 4:18, 19 from Isaiah 61:1, 2 and 58:6]

(He closes the scroll, and sits down in the center of the chancel facing the congregation.) Today this scripture has been fulfilled in your hearing.   *[Luke: 4:21]*

LEADER: A beautiful reading from the prophet. We all long for the coming of that great day.

JESUS: That day has arrived.

LEADER: Are you saying the Lord's anointed has arrived?

JESUS: I'm saying that God has anointed me to this ministry.

FIRST MAN: And when did this take place?

JESUS: Several weeks ago . . . at the river Jordan.

FIRST MAN: And who anointed you?

JESUS: The spirit of God.

FIRST MAN: That isn't what I meant. Who was the person who anointed you?

JESUS: It was during my baptism at the hands of John.

(Some people in the congregation, who have rehearsed earlier, turn to one another in conversation.)

FIRST MAN: But John is baptizing sinners.

JESUS: John is calling for a genuine return to righteousness.

FIRST MAN: And you were unrighteous?

JESUS: Should we not all seek true righteousness?

SECOND MAN: Are you a disciple of John?

JESUS: No. But I respect his work.

SECOND MAN: Is John the long promised Messiah?

JESUS: He doesn't claim to be.

SECOND MAN: Is he Elijah brought back to life?

JESUS: John is preparing the way for the arrival of God's kingdom.

SECOND MAN: Do **you** claim to be the Messiah?

JESUS: I claim God has anointed me to the ministry described by Isaiah.

LEADER: But that **is** the ministry of the Messiah.

JESUS: So be it then.

FIRST MAN: Arrogance! Sheer arrogance! We all know who you are. You're Joseph's son. You're one of us. Your mother and brother and sisters live nearby. How can you make such a claim? If you **are** the anointed of God, give us some proof.

JESUS: You want me to prove my ministry?

FIRST MAN: Yes! We've heard rumors of what you did in Capernaum. Show us and perhaps we'll believe.

JESUS: What kind of sign do you want?

SECOND MAN: Turn a stone to bread. Moses was able to draw water from the rock in Horeb. Surely you should be able to do as much.

JESUS: Man shall not live by bread alone, but by every word that comes from the mouth of God.

SECOND MAN: You're not interested in the material welfare of God's people.

JESUS: I didn't say that. But I refuse to gain the loyalty of people by a miraculous provision of material goods.

SECOND MAN: You separate our material and spiritual needs?

JESUS: Quite the reverse. I **refuse** to separate them by limiting myself to one or the other.

FIRST MAN: But a spectacular miracle could win you the following you need. With such power you might drive the Romans from the land. Who knows? You might gain power over the whole world?

JESUS: I don't want such power. You shall worship the Lord your God. And him only shall you serve.

FIRST MAN: You expect to succeed without some change in our political and economic systems?

JESUS: I didn't say that. I say lasting justice and peace cannot be achieved by power separated from personal integrity.

LEADER: But surely you must offer some sign. Without that how can we be sure you are one called of God? How can you be sure yourself? Give a sign!

JESUS: We are not to test the Lord our God. My ministry must be its own test. You want a sign? The blind recover their sight, the lame walk, the lepers are cleansed, the deaf hear, the dead are raised to life, the poor are hearing the good news. What more do you want?

SECOND MAN: But you're obviously human, like ourselves.

JESUS: Doesn't God work through human flesh?

FIRST MAN: *(with a sneer)* Ordinary people like you?

JESUS: No prophet is accepted in his own country.

FIRST MAN: What do you mean?

JESUS: The prophets of old were often rejected by those who knew them. Jeremiah was imprisoned. Amos was advised to leave town.

FIRST MAN: You're putting yourself in the category of Jeremiah and Amos?

JESUS: I'm saying their work was not always accepted.

LEADER: And you say **your** work is to comfort the sorrowful, encourage the meek, befriend the lonely, heal the blind and lame and deaf, raise the dead and preach God's good news to the poor?

JESUS: Yes.

LEADER: Quite an ambitious undertaking.

FIRST MAN: And soon the whole world will be transformed?

JESUS: I don't expect an easy path. The servant of God may be despised and rejected; a man of sorrows, and acquainted with grief.

SECOND MAN: You said earlier that you were baptized by John.

JESUS: Yes.

SECOND MAN: You obviously feel he is a man of God.

JESUS: Among those born of women none is greater than John.

SECOND MAN: And yet with such credentials John isn't the Messiah?

JESUS: John prepares the way for the coming of God's kingdom. He is a very humble man. He who is least in the kingdom of God is greater than John.

SECOND MAN: Do you share John's attitude to Gentile people?

JESUS: That they too can be received into God's kingdom?

SECOND MAN: That isn't what I meant. You know that Judaism makes provision for the reception of Gentiles.

JESUS: Through a very elaborate process of purification.

SECOND MAN: Correct. John seems to have rejected that procedure.

JESUS: He calls for repentance and a baptism representing God's cleansing.

LEADER: True. But John's baptism is different from our proselyte baptism.

JESUS: Because he calls us to baptism as well?

LEADER: Precisely. He destroys the difference.

JESUS: There is a difference?

FIRST MAN: Of course there's a difference. How can you deny the past history of your people?

JESUS: I'm not denying our past history. But are we any more righteous than other people?

SECOND MAN: We don't deny the need to repent. But proselyte baptism symbolizes the need for serious purification.

JESUS: And you don't think we have such need?

SECOND MAN: *(with annoyance)* Are you one of those strange Essenes who think we need to be baptized every day?

JESUS: I don't call for that.

SECOND MAN: I'm relieved. But you won't admit that John is a religious fanatic?

(There is noise in the congregation to indicate not all share this view of John.)

JESUS: If I were to say that, I'd have to reject many of the prophets.

FIRST MAN: But who before John has suggested that Jew and non-Jew stand equal before God?

JESUS: Have you heard of Elijah?

FIRST MAN: *(with annoyance)* Of course we have.

JESUS: Have you heard, "There were many widows in Israel in the days of Elijah, when the heaven was shut up three years and six months, when there came a great famine over all the land." [*Luke 4:25*]

FIRST MAN: Yes.

JESUS: To whom was Elijah sent?

FIRST MAN: To Zarephath.

JESUS: In the land of Sidon.

FIRST MAN: Yes.

JESUS: A Gentile. *(murmur in the congregation)* And have you heard of Elisha? *(silence)* There were many lepers in Israel in the time of the prophet Elisha. And who was cleansed? *(silence)* Who?

SECOND MAN: *(reluctantly)* Naaman.

JESUS: The Syrian. . . . Another Gentile.

LEADER: You mean to say you're going to reject your own people and minister to the Gentiles.

JESUS: Not at all. I'm Jewish and I'm called to minister to my own people. I don't intend to proselytize the Gentiles. But neither do I deny that the grace of God can be at work in their lives.

LEADER: That is very generous, young man. But it threatens the very foundation of our faith.

JESUS: I think not. It is a fulfillment of the deepest conviction of our faith. Joel promised that one day God would pour out his spirit upon all flesh.

FIRST MAN: He was speaking to our people.

JESUS: It is a light thing that you should be my servant to raise up the tribes of Jacob, and to restore the preserved of Israel. I will also give you for a light to the Gentiles, that you may be my salvation unto the end of the earth.

(Individuals in the congregation stand, one after another in a growing crescendo.)

Blasphemy!

Throw him out!

Such arrogance!

Kill him!

(The Leader hurries to stand between Jesus and the angry congregation, raising his arms to pacify them. When the noise has subsided, he turns about to Jesus.)

LEADER: I think perhaps you should leave.

JESUS: You're right. I have offended some. But blessed is the man who is not offended in me. I speak the truth in love and will force no one. Shalom! *(He slowly walks the length of the church and out.)*

The Last Meal

TIME: The night before the crucifixion of Jesus

PLACE: A room with a table in the center. On it are a jug of wine, a goblet, a loaf of bread, a tray of herbs, and candles. Nearby a towel is draped over a stool beside a basin of water.

CHARACTERS: Judas
       Peter
       James
       John
       Jesus

(Onto a darkened stage a man gropes with a taper in hand. Four others follow. The first lights the candles.)

JUDAS: Very pleasant, Peter. You've done a good job.

PETER: John should share the credit.

JAMES: We're fortunate to get such a spacious room.

JOHN: Especially at Passover.

JUDAS: Who owns the room?

JOHN: A friend of Jesus.

JUDAS: A follower?

PETER: A sympathizer.

JUDAS: *(with a sneer)* Another hidden disciple!

JOHN: Don't be too harsh, Judas.

JUDAS: No? If we were more decisive I'm sure many more would join us openly. Instead we seem to be losing strength.

JAMES: You forget the entry into Jerusalem.

PETER: That was some show!

JUDAS: People are fickle. Up one day . . . down the next. If we don't make a move soon we won't hold them.

JAMES: Perhaps you're right Judas. *(turning to Jesus)* Master, isn't it time to establish the kingdom?

JESUS: The kingdom of God is being established.

JUDAS: But when do we make our move? When do we take power?

JESUS: I'm afraid you still misunderstand me.

PETER: Judas, you're too worried about finances. Even if we must struggle some more, I'm with the Master all the way.

JOHN: But Judas has a point. We can't go on like this much longer.

PETER: Like what?

JOHN: Teaching and healing, traveling around . . .

JUDAS: Without making a move to challenge the power structure.

PETER: But how, Judas? How?

JUDAS: You know my position.

JOHN: Armed rebellion isn't feasible. We aren't strong enough.

JUDAS: We won't get any stronger if we continue to lose support. Make a move and people will rise up . . . the way they did last Sunday.

JESUS: Power! Power! That's all you think about. I've so wanted to celebrate this Passover with you, and all you can talk about is power.

JUDAS: Evasion! . . . always evasion!

PETER: That's enough, Judas.

JOHN: No, Judas is right. We need to discuss the matter. We need a provisional government.

JUDAS: With James and John at the top, I suppose.

JAMES: I can think of no two better.

JUDAS: Just because your father's a prosperous fisherman.

JOHN: A little more business sense might not hurt you.

JUDAS: Are you insinuating I'm not honest.

JOHN: No. Just a little inefficient.

JUDAS: I'd like to see you balance the budget with dropping support.

JAMES: I'd start by cutting our givings to the poor.

JUDAS: And spend it on costly ointment?

PETER: We've been over that before.

JUDAS: He started it. I don't want two loudmouths in charge.

JAMES: Class! Social class is what we offer!

PETER: Class. That's a joke. Just because Zebedee did well at fishing, you think you own Galilee.

JAMES: At least we're better fishermen. That should count for something in this motly crew.

JESUS: Would you all listen a moment?

JUDAS: *(with a sneer)* Another lecture?

JESUS: On power. How many times have I insisted that the kingdom won't be established by lording it over one another.

JOHN: But someone must be in charge.

PETER: As long as it isn't you or James!

JUDAS: I agree that some decisive leadership is needed.

PETER: And you don't think Jesus has it?

JUDAS: He could be more decisive.

JOHN: I'm not complaining about the Master's leadership. But he needs some help. Someone should be second-in-command.

JESUS: *(He goes over, picks up a basin and pours some water into it.)* What do I have here?

PETER: A basin.

JAMES: Filled with water.

JESUS: And what is it for?

JOHN: Washing dusty feet.

JESUS: Precisely. *(Going over to Peter, He prepares to take off his sandals.)*

PETER: Oh no, Master, not me. You're not my servant. I can wash my own feet.

JESUS: You won't allow this courtesy?

PETER: It's not that. I should be doing it for **you**.

JESUS: Why?

PETER: Because you're the leader.

JESUS: And what does it mean if I the leader want to wash your feet?

PETER: I don't understand.

JUDAS: *(with a sneer)* This is true greatness . . . the ability to serve one another.

JESUS: Yes, Judas. But why the sneer? I don't feel I lose my dignity in this act. I express my love. If Peter won't let me wash his feet, he can't understand me.

PETER: I'm sorry, Master. If that's the way you feel, you can wash all of me.

JESUS: That's not necessary. It's the attitude, not the act.

JUDAS: So the kingdom will come as everyone goes around washing feet. If the army can't fight, at least it will have clean feet.

(There is an awkward silence. The disciples glare at Judas as if his sarcasm has gone too far.)

JESUS: I think it's time to eat. *(They take their places with Jesus in the center; Peter on his immediate right; Judas on the far right; John on the immediate left of Jesus and James on the far left, all facing the audience. If a note of realism is desired the participants could recline in white robes on cushions around a low table. Jesus pours wine into a goblet.)* Praise to You, our God, for creating the fruit of the vine. Take this and share it. *(The goblet is passed around; then a tray of herbs.)*

JAMES: Why is this night different from all other nights?

JESUS: It is the sacrifice of the Lord's Passover for he passed over the houses of the people of Israel in Egypt when he slew the Egyptians.

PETER: Praise the Lord!

JOHN: God be praised!

JUDAS: Praise the name of the Lord!

JAMES: Blessed be the name of the Lord from this time forth and for evermore!

PETER: From the rising of the sun to its setting the name of the Lord is to be praised!

JOHN: The Lord is high above all nations, and his glory above the heavens!

JUDAS: Who is like the Lord our God, who is seated on high, who looks far down upon the heavens and the earth?

JAMES: He raises the poor from the dust, and lifts the needy from the ash heap, to make them sit with princes.

ALL: Praise the Lord! [Psalm 113: 1-9]

(Jesus pours a second goblet of wine and passes it around. Then he picks up a piece of bread.)

JESUS: This is the bread provided by God. It represents my body given up for your sake. Take and eat! *(They pass the bread around.)*

PETER: What do you mean saying your body given for us?

JESUS: I'm referring to my coming sufferings.

JAMES: What sufferings?

JESUS: The sufferings I've spoken of for the last several weeks. The true servant of God must suffer many things.

PETER: Don't worry. We'll protect you.

JESUS: From whom?

PETER: Your enemies, of course?

JESUS: And who will protect me from you?

JOHN: From us?

JESUS: Yes. I will be betrayed by one of you.

JAMES: Impossible. None of us would do such a thing. *(They all join in a chorus of denial.)*

JESUS: *(as Judas reaches over to tray of herbs)* The hardest blow is to be betrayed by someone who dips his hand into the same bowl. *(Judas pauses for an instant and then continues.)*

PETER: If everyone else forsakes you, I'll remain faithful . . . even to death.

JESUS: Peter, Satan will sift you like flour. Before the cock heralds the coming day you will deny me more than once.

PETER: Never!

JESUS: I pray that God will sustain you.

JOHN: We've had our differences and sometimes grown impatient but none of us would deny you. We believe you **will** establish God's kingdom.

JESUS: You don't seem to understand how the kingdom will be established.

PETER: We're willing to wait.

JESUS: It's not a matter of time; it's a question of method. What would you say if I told you to go out and buy weapons.

JUDAS: No need. Here are two swords. *(He draws out two short swords. Peter takes one.)*

JESUS: You wouldn't sense any inconsistency?

JUDAS: Not at all. That's the only power Rome understands.

JOHN: There's no need for arms. God will overturn the Romans.

JUDAS: While we sit around and talk.

JAMES: With God all things are possible!

JUDAS: But not probable.

JESUS: The kingdom is closer than you imagine. *(He pours out another goblet of wine.)* This wine represents my life's blood poured out for you in covenant. *(The goblet is passed around.)* I shall not drink again of the fruit of the vine until that day when I drink it new in the kingdom of God.

PETER: *(with surprise)* That soon?

JESUS: That soon!

JAMES: That's what we've been waiting for. *(He stands.)* This calls for a celebration!

PETER: *(also standing)* Let's join in the closing Psalm.

JESUS: O give thanks to the Lord, for he is good.

ALL: His steadfast love endures forever!

PETER: Let Israel say, "His steadfast love endures for ever."

JAMES: Let the house of Aaron say, "His steadfast love endures for ever."

JOHN: Let those who fear the Lord say, "His steadfast love endures for ever."

JESUS: Out of my distress I called on the Lord; the Lord answered me and set me free.

PETER: With the Lord on my side I do not fear. What can [people] do to me?

JUDAS: The Lord is on my side to help me; I shall look in triumph on those who hate me.

JAMES: It is better to take refuge in the Lord than to put confidence in [flesh].

JOHN: It is better to take refuge in the Lord than to put confidence in princes.

[Psalm 118:1-9]

JESUS: I thank You that You have answered me and become my salvation. The stone which the builders rejected has become the head of the corner.

ALL: This is the Lord's doing; it is marvelous in our eyes. This is the day which the Lord has made. Let us rejoice and be glad in it. *[Psalm 118:21-24]*

(They blow out the candles and leave by the light of a taper.)

The Last Meal

TIME: The night before the crucifixion of Jesus

PLACE: A room with a table in the center. On it are a jug of wine, a goblet, a loaf of bread, a tray of herbs, and candles. Nearby a towel is draped over a stool beside a basin of water.

CHARACTERS: Judas
                   Peter
                   James
                   John
                   Jesus

(Onto a darkened stage a man gropes with a taper in hand. Four others follow. The first lights the candles.)

JUDAS: Very pleasant, Peter. You've done a good job.

PETER: John should share the credit.

JAMES: We're fortunate to get such a spacious room.

JOHN: Especially at Passover.

JUDAS: Who owns the room?

JOHN: A friend of Jesus.

JUDAS: A follower?

PETER: A sympathizer.

JUDAS: *(with a sneer)* Another hidden disciple!

JOHN: Don't be too harsh, Judas.

JUDAS: No? If we were more decisive I'm sure many more would join us openly. Instead we seem to be losing strength.

JAMES: You forget the entry into Jerusalem.

PETER: That was some show!

JUDAS: People are fickle. Up one day . . . down the next. If we don't make a move soon we won't hold them.

JAMES: Perhaps you're right Judas. *(turning to Jesus)* Master, isn't it time to establish the kingdom?

JESUS: The kingdom of God is being established.

JUDAS: But when do we make our move? When do we take power?

JESUS: I'm afraid you still misunderstand me.

PETER: Judas, you're too worried about finances. Even if we must struggle some more, I'm with the Master all the way.

JOHN: But Judas has a point. We can't go on like this much longer.

PETER: Like what?

JOHN: Teaching and healing, traveling around . . .

JUDAS: Without making a move to challenge the power structure.

PETER: But how, Judas? How?

JUDAS: You know my position.

JOHN: Armed rebellion isn't feasible. We aren't strong enough.

JUDAS: We won't get any stronger if we continue to lose support. Make a move and people will rise up . . . the way they did last Sunday.

JESUS: Power! Power! That's all you think about. I've so wanted to celebrate this Passover with you, and all you can talk about is power.

JUDAS: Evasion! . . . always evasion!

PETER: That's enough, Judas.

JOHN: No, Judas is right. We need to discuss the matter. We need a provisional government.

JUDAS: With James and John at the top, I suppose.

JAMES: I can think of no two better.

JUDAS: Just because your father's a prosperous fisherman.

JOHN: A little more business sense might not hurt you.

JUDAS: Are you insinuating I'm not honest.

JOHN: No. Just a little inefficient.

JUDAS: I'd like to see you balance the budget with dropping support.

JAMES: I'd start by cutting our givings to the poor.

JUDAS: And spend it on costly ointment?

PETER: We've been over that before.

JUDAS: He started it. I don't want two loudmouths in charge.

JAMES: Class! Social class is what we offer!

PETER: Class. That's a joke. Just because Zebedee did well at fishing, you think you own Galilee.

JAMES: At least we're better fishermen. That should count for something in this motly crew.

JESUS: Would you all listen a moment?

JUDAS: *(with a sneer)* Another lecture?

JESUS: On power. How many times have I insisted that the kingdom won't be established by lording it over one another.

JOHN: But someone must be in charge.

PETER: As long as it isn't you or James!

JUDAS: I agree that some decisive leadership is needed.

PETER: And you don't think Jesus has it?

JUDAS: He could be more decisive.

JOHN: I'm not complaining about the Master's leadership. But he needs some help. Someone should be second-in-command.

JESUS: *(He goes over, picks up a basin and pours some water into it.)* What do I have here?

PETER: A basin.

JAMES: Filled with water.

JESUS: And what is it for?

JOHN: Washing dusty feet.

JESUS: Precisely. *(Going over to Peter, He prepares to take off his sandals.)*

PETER: Oh no, Master, not me. You're not my servant. I can wash my own feet.

JESUS: You won't allow this courtesy?

PETER: It's not that. I should be doing it for **you**.

JESUS: Why?

PETER: Because you're the leader.

JESUS: And what does it mean if I the leader want to wash your feet?

PETER: I don't understand.

JUDAS: *(with a sneer)* This is true greatness . . . the ability to serve one another.

JESUS: Yes, Judas. But why the sneer? I don't feel I lose my dignity in this act. I express my love. If Peter won't let me wash his feet, he can't understand me.

PETER: I'm sorry, Master. If that's the way you feel, you can wash all of me.

JESUS: That's not necessary. It's the attitude, not the act.

JUDAS: So the kingdom will come as everyone goes around washing feet. If the army can't fight, at least it will have clean feet.

(There is an awkward silence. The disciples glare at Judas as if his sarcasm has gone too far.)

JESUS: I think it's time to eat. *(They take their places with Jesus in the center; Peter on his immediate right; Judas on the far right; John on the immediate left of Jesus and James on the far left, all facing the audience. If a note of realism is desired the participants could recline in white robes on cushions around a low table. Jesus pours wine into a goblet.)* Praise to You, our God, for creating the fruit of the vine. Take this and share it. *(The goblet is passed around; then a tray of herbs.)*

JAMES: Why is this night different from all other nights?

JESUS: It is the sacrifice of the Lord's Passover for he passed over the houses of the people of Israel in Egypt when he slew the Egyptians.

PETER: Praise the Lord!

JOHN: God be praised!

JUDAS: Praise the name of the Lord!

JAMES: Blessed be the name of the Lord from this time forth and for evermore!

PETER: From the rising of the sun to its setting the name of the Lord is to be praised!

JOHN: The Lord is high above all nations, and his glory above the heavens!

JUDAS: Who is like the Lord our God, who is seated on high, who looks far down upon the heavens and the earth?

JAMES: He raises the poor from the dust, and lifts the needy from the ash heap, to make them sit with princes.

ALL: Praise the Lord! [Psalm 113: 1-9]

(Jesus pours a second goblet of wine and passes it around. Then he picks up a piece of bread.)

JESUS: This is the bread provided by God. It represents my body given up for your sake. Take and eat! *(They pass the bread around.)*

PETER: What do you mean saying your body given for us?

JESUS: I'm referring to my coming sufferings.

JAMES: What sufferings?

JESUS: The sufferings I've spoken of for the last several weeks. The true servant of God must suffer many things.

PETER: Don't worry. We'll protect you.

JESUS: From whom?

PETER: Your enemies, of course?

JESUS: And who will protect me from you?

JOHN: From us?

JESUS: Yes. I will be betrayed by one of you.

JAMES: Impossible. None of us would do such a thing. *(They all join in a chorus of denial.)*

JESUS: *(as Judas reaches over to tray of herbs)* The hardest blow is to be betrayed by someone who dips his hand into the same bowl. *(Judas pauses for an instant and then continues.)*

PETER: If everyone else forsakes you, I'll remain faithful . . . even to death.

JESUS: Peter, Satan will sift you like flour. Before the cock heralds the coming day you will deny me more than once.

PETER: Never!

JESUS: I pray that God will sustain you.

JOHN: We've had our differences and sometimes grown impatient but none of us would deny you. We believe you **will** establish God's kingdom.

JESUS: You don't seem to understand how the kingdom will be established.

PETER: We're willing to wait.

JESUS: It's not a matter of time; it's a question of method. What would you say if I told you to go out and buy weapons.

JUDAS: No need. Here are two swords. *(He draws out two short swords. Peter takes one.)*

JESUS: You wouldn't sense any inconsistency?

JUDAS: Not at all. That's the only power Rome understands.

JOHN: There's no need for arms. God will overturn the Romans.

JUDAS: While we sit around and talk.

JAMES: With God all things are possible!

JUDAS: But not probable.

JESUS: The kingdom is closer than you imagine. *(He pours out another goblet of wine.)* This wine represents my life's blood poured out for you in covenant. *(The goblet is passed around.)* I shall not drink again of the fruit of the vine until that day when I drink it new in the kingdom of God.

PETER: *(with surprise)* That soon?

JESUS: That soon!

JAMES: That's what we've been waiting for. *(He stands.)* This calls for a celebration!

PETER: *(also standing)* Let's join in the closing Psalm.

JESUS: O give thanks to the Lord, for he is good.

ALL: His steadfast love endures forever!

PETER: Let Israel say, "His steadfast love endures for ever."

JAMES: Let the house of Aaron say, "His steadfast love endures for ever."

JOHN: Let those who fear the Lord say, "His steadfast love endures for ever."

JESUS: Out of my distress I called on the Lord; the Lord answered me and set me free.

PETER: With the Lord on my side I do not fear. What can [people] do to me?

JUDAS: The Lord is on my side to help me; I shall look in triumph on those who hate me.

JAMES: It is better to take refuge in the Lord than to put confidence in [flesh].

JOHN: It is better to take refuge in the Lord than to put confidence in princes.

[Psalm 118:1-9]

JESUS: I thank You that You have answered me and become my salvation. The stone which the builders rejected has become the head of the corner.

ALL: This is the Lord's doing; it is marvelous in our eyes. This is the day which the Lord has made. Let us rejoice and be glad in it. [Psalm 118:21-24]

(They blow out the candles and leave by the light of a taper.)

The Last Meal

TIME: The night before the crucifixion of Jesus

PLACE: A room with a table in the center. On it are a jug of wine, a goblet, a loaf of bread, a tray of herbs, and candles. Nearby a towel is draped over a stool beside a basin of water.

CHARACTERS: Judas
             Peter
             James
             John
             Jesus

(Onto a darkened stage a man gropes with a taper in hand. Four others follow. The first lights the candles.)

JUDAS: Very pleasant, Peter. You've done a good job.

PETER: John should share the credit.

JAMES: We're fortunate to get such a spacious room.

JOHN: Especially at Passover.

JUDAS: Who owns the room?

JOHN: A friend of Jesus.

JUDAS: A follower?

PETER: A sympathizer.

JUDAS: *(with a sneer)* Another hidden disciple!

JOHN: Don't be too harsh, Judas.

JUDAS: No? If we were more decisive I'm sure many more would join us openly. Instead we seem to be losing strength.

JAMES: You forget the entry into Jerusalem.

PETER: That was some show!

JUDAS: People are fickle. Up one day . . . down the next. If we don't make a move soon we won't hold them.

JAMES: Perhaps you're right Judas. *(turning to Jesus)* Master, isn't it time to establish the kingdom?

JESUS: The kingdom of God is being established.

JUDAS: But when do we make our move? When do we take power?

JESUS: I'm afraid you still misunderstand me.

PETER: Judas, you're too worried about finances. Even if we must struggle some more, I'm with the Master all the way.

JOHN: But Judas has a point. We can't go on like this much longer.

PETER: Like what?

JOHN: Teaching and healing, traveling around . . .

JUDAS: Without making a move to challenge the power structure.

PETER: But how, Judas? How?

JUDAS: You know my position.

JOHN: Armed rebellion isn't feasible. We aren't strong enough.

JUDAS: We won't get any stronger if we continue to lose support. Make a move and people will rise up . . . the way they did last Sunday.

JESUS: Power! Power! That's all you think about. I've so wanted to celebrate this Passover with you, and all you can talk about is power.

JUDAS: Evasion! . . . always evasion!

PETER: That's enough, Judas.

JOHN: No, Judas is right. We need to discuss the matter. We need a provisional government.

JUDAS: With James and John at the top, I suppose.

JAMES: I can think of no two better.

JUDAS: Just because your father's a prosperous fisherman.

JOHN: A little more business sense might not hurt you.

JUDAS: Are you insinuating I'm not honest.

JOHN: No. Just a little inefficient.

JUDAS: I'd like to see you balance the budget with dropping support.

JAMES: I'd start by cutting our givings to the poor.

JUDAS: And spend it on costly ointment?

PETER: We've been over that before.

JUDAS: He started it. I don't want two loudmouths in charge.

JAMES: Class! Social class is what we offer!

PETER: Class. That's a joke. Just because Zebedee did well at fishing, you think you own Galilee.

JAMES: At least we're better fishermen. That should count for something in this motly crew.

JESUS: Would you all listen a moment?

JUDAS: *(with a sneer)* Another lecture?

JESUS: On power. How many times have I insisted that the kingdom won't be established by lording it over one another.

JOHN: But someone must be in charge.

PETER: As long as it isn't you or James!

JUDAS: I agree that some decisive leadership is needed.

PETER: And you don't think Jesus has it?

JUDAS: He could be more decisive.

JOHN: I'm not complaining about the Master's leadership. But he needs some help. Someone should be second-in-command.

JESUS: *(He goes over, picks up a basin and pours some water into it.)* What do I have here?

PETER: A basin.

JAMES: Filled with water.

JESUS: And what is it for?

JOHN: Washing dusty feet.

JESUS: Precisely. *(Going over to Peter, He prepares to take off his sandals.)*

PETER: Oh no, Master, not me. You're not my servant. I can wash my own feet.

JESUS: You won't allow this courtesy?

PETER: It's not that. I should be doing it for **you**.

JESUS: Why?

PETER: Because you're the leader.

JESUS: And what does it mean if I the leader want to wash your feet?

PETER: I don't understand.

JUDAS: *(with a sneer)* This is true greatness . . . the ability to serve one another.

JESUS: Yes, Judas. But why the sneer? I don't feel I lose my dignity in this act. I express my love. If Peter won't let me wash his feet, he can't understand me.

PETER: I'm sorry, Master. If that's the way you feel, you can wash all of me.

JESUS: That's not necessary. It's the attitude, not the act.

JUDAS: So the kingdom will come as everyone goes around washing feet. If the army can't fight, at least it will have clean feet.

(There is an awkward silence. The disciples glare at Judas as if his sarcasm has gone too far.)

JESUS: I think it's time to eat. *(They take their places with Jesus in the center; Peter on his immediate right; Judas on the far right; John on the immediate left of Jesus and James on the far left, all facing the audience. If a note of realism is desired the participants could recline in white robes on cushions around a low table. Jesus pours wine into a goblet.)* Praise to You, our God, for creating the fruit of the vine. Take this and share it. *(The goblet is passed around; then a tray of herbs.)*

JAMES: Why is this night different from all other nights?

JESUS: It is the sacrifice of the Lord's Passover for he passed over the houses of the people of Israel in Egypt when he slew the Egyptians.

PETER: Praise the Lord!

JOHN: God be praised!

JUDAS: Praise the name of the Lord!

JAMES: Blessed be the name of the Lord from this time forth and for evermore!

PETER: From the rising of the sun to its setting the name of the Lord is to be praised!

JOHN: The Lord is high above all nations, and his glory above the heavens!

JUDAS: Who is like the Lord our God, who is seated on high, who looks far down upon the heavens and the earth?

JAMES: He raises the poor from the dust, and lifts the needy from the ash heap, to make them sit with princes.

ALL: Praise the Lord!   *[Psalm 113: 1-9]*

(Jesus pours a second goblet of wine and passes it around. Then he picks up a piece of bread.)

JESUS: This is the bread provided by God. It represents my body given up for your sake. Take and eat! *(They pass the bread around.)*

PETER: What do you mean saying your body given for us?

JESUS: I'm referring to my coming sufferings.

JAMES: What sufferings?

JESUS: The sufferings I've spoken of for the last several weeks. The true servant of God must suffer many things.

PETER: Don't worry. We'll protect you.

JESUS: From whom?

PETER: Your enemies, of course?

JESUS: And who will protect me from you?

JOHN: From us?

JESUS: Yes. I will be betrayed by one of you.

JAMES: Impossible. None of us would do such a thing. *(They all join in a chorus of denial.)*

JESUS: *(as Judas reaches over to tray of herbs)* The hardest blow is to be betrayed by someone who dips his hand into the same bowl. *(Judas pauses for an instant and then continues.)*

PETER: If everyone else forsakes you, I'll remain faithful . . . even to death.

JESUS: Peter, Satan will sift you like flour. Before the cock heralds the coming day you will deny me more than once.

PETER: Never!

JESUS: I pray that God will sustain you.

JOHN: We've had our differences and sometimes grown impatient but none of us would deny you. We believe you **will** establish God's kingdom.

JESUS: You don't seem to understand how the kingdom will be established.

PETER: We're willing to wait.

JESUS: It's not a matter of time; it's a question of method. What would you say if I told you to go out and buy weapons.

JUDAS: No need. Here are two swords. *(He draws out two short swords. Peter takes one.)*

JESUS: You wouldn't sense any inconsistency?

JUDAS: Not at all. That's the only power Rome understands.

JOHN: There's no need for arms. God will overturn the Romans.

JUDAS: While we sit around and talk.

JAMES: With God all things are possible!

JUDAS: But not probable.

JESUS: The kingdom is closer than you imagine. *(He pours out another goblet of wine.)* This wine represents my life's blood poured out for you in covenant. *(The goblet is passed around.)* I shall not drink again of the fruit of the vine until that day when I drink it new in the kingdom of God.

PETER: *(with surprise)* That soon?

JESUS: That soon!

JAMES: That's what we've been waiting for. *(He stands.)* This calls for a celebration!

PETER: *(also standing)* Let's join in the closing Psalm.

JESUS: O give thanks to the Lord, for he is good.

ALL: His steadfast love endures forever!

PETER: Let Israel say, "His steadfast love endures for ever."

JAMES: Let the house of Aaron say, "His steadfast love endures for ever."

JOHN: Let those who fear the Lord say, "His steadfast love endures for ever."

JESUS: Out of my distress I called on the Lord; the Lord answered me and set me free.

PETER: With the Lord on my side I do not fear. What can [people] do to me?

JUDAS: The Lord is on my side to help me; I shall look in triumph on those who hate me.

JAMES: It is better to take refuge in the Lord than to put confidence in [flesh].

JOHN: It is better to take refuge in the Lord than to put confidence in princes.

[*Psalm 118:1-9*]

JESUS: I thank You that You have answered me and become my salvation. The stone which the builders rejected has become the head of the corner.

ALL: This is the Lord's doing; it is marvelous in our eyes. This is the day which the Lord has made. Let us rejoice and be glad in it. [*Psalm 118:21-24*]

(They blow out the candles and leave by the light of a taper.)

The Last Meal

TIME: The night before the crucifixion of Jesus

PLACE: A room with a table in the center. On it are a jug of wine, a goblet, a loaf of bread, a tray of herbs, and candles. Nearby a towel is draped over a stool beside a basin of water.

CHARACTERS: Judas
                 Peter
                 James
                 John
                 Jesus

(Onto a darkened stage a man gropes with a taper in hand. Four others follow. The first lights the candles.)

JUDAS: Very pleasant, Peter. You've done a good job.

PETER: John should share the credit.

JAMES: We're fortunate to get such a spacious room.

JOHN: Especially at Passover.

JUDAS: Who owns the room?

JOHN: A friend of Jesus.

JUDAS: A follower?

PETER: A sympathizer.

JUDAS: *(with a sneer)* Another hidden disciple!

JOHN: Don't be too harsh, Judas.

JUDAS: No? If we were more decisive I'm sure many more would join us openly. Instead we seem to be losing strength.

JAMES: You forget the entry into Jerusalem.

PETER: That was some show!

JUDAS: People are fickle. Up one day . . . down the next. If we don't make a move soon we won't hold them.

JAMES: Perhaps you're right Judas. *(turning to Jesus)* Master, isn't it time to establish the kingdom?

JESUS: The kingdom of God is being established.

JUDAS: But when do we make our move? When do we take power?

JESUS: I'm afraid you still misunderstand me.

PETER: Judas, you're too worried about finances. Even if we must struggle some more, I'm with the Master all the way.

JOHN: But Judas has a point. We can't go on like this much longer.

PETER: Like what?

JOHN: Teaching and healing, traveling around . . .

JUDAS: Without making a move to challenge the power structure.

PETER: But how, Judas? How?

JUDAS: You know my position.

JOHN: Armed rebellion isn't feasible. We aren't strong enough.

JUDAS: We won't get any stronger if we continue to lose support. Make a move and people will rise up . . . the way they did last Sunday.

JESUS: Power! Power! That's all you think about. I've so wanted to celebrate this Passover with you, and all you can talk about is power.

JUDAS: Evasion! . . . always evasion!

PETER: That's enough, Judas.

JOHN: No, Judas is right. We need to discuss the matter. We need a provisional government.

JUDAS: With James and John at the top, I suppose.

JAMES: I can think of no two better.

JUDAS: Just because your father's a prosperous fisherman.

JOHN: A little more business sense might not hurt you.

JUDAS: Are you insinuating I'm not honest.

JOHN: No. Just a little inefficient.

JUDAS: I'd like to see you balance the budget with dropping support.

JAMES: I'd start by cutting our givings to the poor.

JUDAS: And spend it on costly ointment?

PETER: We've been over that before.

JUDAS: He started it. I don't want two loudmouths in charge.

JAMES: Class! Social class is what we offer!

PETER: Class. That's a joke. Just because Zebedee did well at fishing, you think you own Galilee.

JAMES: At least we're better fishermen. That should count for something in this motly crew.

JESUS: Would you all listen a moment?

JUDAS: *(with a sneer)* Another lecture?

JESUS: On power. How many times have I insisted that the kingdom won't be established by lording it over one another.

JOHN: But someone must be in charge.

PETER: As long as it isn't you or James!

JUDAS: I agree that some decisive leadership is needed.

PETER: And you don't think Jesus has it?

JUDAS: He could be more decisive.

JOHN: I'm not complaining about the Master's leadership. But he needs some help. Someone should be second-in-command.

JESUS: *(He goes over, picks up a basin and pours some water into it.)* What do I have here?

PETER: A basin.

JAMES: Filled with water.

JESUS: And what is it for?

JOHN: Washing dusty feet.

JESUS: Precisely. *(Going over to Peter, He prepares to take off his sandals.)*

PETER: Oh no, Master, not me. You're not my servant. I can wash my own feet.

JESUS: You won't allow this courtesy?

PETER: It's not that. I should be doing it for **you**.

JESUS: Why?

PETER: Because you're the leader.

JESUS: And what does it mean if I the leader want to wash your feet?

PETER: I don't understand.

JUDAS: *(with a sneer)* This is true greatness . . . the ability to serve one another.

JESUS: Yes, Judas. But why the sneer? I don't feel I lose my dignity in this act. I express my love. If Peter won't let me wash his feet, he can't understand me.

PETER: I'm sorry, Master. If that's the way you feel, you can wash all of me.

JESUS: That's not necessary. It's the attitude, not the act.

JUDAS: So the kingdom will come as everyone goes around washing feet. If the army can't fight, at least it will have clean feet.

(There is an awkward silence. The disciples glare at Judas as if his sarcasm has gone too far.)

JESUS: I think it's time to eat. *(They take their places with Jesus in the center; Peter on his immediate right; Judas on the far right; John on the immediate left of Jesus and James on the far left, all facing the audience. If a note of realism is desired the participants could recline in white robes on cushions around a low table. Jesus pours wine into a goblet.)* Praise to You, our God, for creating the fruit of the vine. Take this and share it. *(The goblet is passed around; then a tray of herbs.)*

JAMES: Why is this night different from all other nights?

JESUS: It is the sacrifice of the Lord's Passover for he passed over the houses of the people of Israel in Egypt when he slew the Egyptians.

PETER: Praise the Lord!

JOHN: God be praised!

JUDAS: Praise the name of the Lord!

JAMES: Blessed be the name of the Lord from this time forth and for evermore!

PETER: From the rising of the sun to its setting the name of the Lord is to be praised!

JOHN: The Lord is high above all nations, and his glory above the heavens!

JUDAS: Who is like the Lord our God, who is seated on high, who looks far down upon the heavens and the earth?

JAMES: He raises the poor from the dust, and lifts the needy from the ash heap, to make them sit with princes.

ALL: Praise the Lord! [*Psalm 113: 1-9*]

(Jesus pours a second goblet of wine and passes it around. Then he picks up a piece of bread.)

JESUS: This is the bread provided by God. It represents my body given up for your sake. Take and eat! *(They pass the bread around.)*

PETER: What do you mean saying your body given for us?

JESUS: I'm referring to my coming sufferings.

JAMES: What sufferings?

JESUS: The sufferings I've spoken of for the last several weeks. The true servant of God must suffer many things.

PETER: Don't worry. We'll protect you.

JESUS: From whom?

PETER: Your enemies, of course?

JESUS: And who will protect me from you?

JOHN: From us?

JESUS: Yes. I will be betrayed by one of you.

JAMES: Impossible. None of us would do such a thing. *(They all join in a chorus of denial.)*

JESUS: *(as Judas reaches over to tray of herbs)* The hardest blow is to be betrayed by someone who dips his hand into the same bowl. *(Judas pauses for an instant and then continues.)*

PETER: If everyone else forsakes you, I'll remain faithful . . . even to death.

JESUS: Peter, Satan will sift you like flour. Before the cock heralds the coming day you will deny me more than once.

PETER: Never!

JESUS: I pray that God will sustain you.

JOHN: We've had our differences and sometimes grown impatient but none of us would deny you. We believe you **will** establish God's kingdom.

JESUS: You don't seem to understand how the kingdom will be established.

PETER: We're willing to wait.

JESUS: It's not a matter of time; it's a question of method. What would you say if I told you to go out and buy weapons.

JUDAS: No need. Here are two swords. *(He draws out two short swords. Peter takes one.)*

JESUS: You wouldn't sense any inconsistency?

JUDAS: Not at all. That's the only power Rome understands.

JOHN: There's no need for arms. God will overturn the Romans.

JUDAS: While we sit around and talk.

JAMES: With God all things are possible!

JUDAS: But not probable.

JESUS: The kingdom is closer than you imagine. *(He pours out another goblet of wine.)* This wine represents my life's blood poured out for you in covenant. *(The goblet is passed around.)* I shall not drink again of the fruit of the vine until that day when I drink it new in the kingdom of God.

PETER: *(with surprise)* That soon?

JESUS: That soon!

JAMES: That's what we've been waiting for. *(He stands.)* This calls for a celebration!

PETER: *(also standing)* Let's join in the closing Psalm.

JESUS: O give thanks to the Lord, for he is good.

ALL: His steadfast love endures forever!

PETER: Let Israel say, "His steadfast love endures for ever."

JAMES: Let the house of Aaron say, "His steadfast love endures for ever."

JOHN: Let those who fear the Lord say, "His steadfast love endures for ever."

JESUS: Out of my distress I called on the Lord; the Lord answered me and set me free.

PETER: With the Lord on my side I do not fear. What can [people] do to me?

JUDAS: The Lord is on my side to help me; I shall look in triumph on those who hate me.

JAMES: It is better to take refuge in the Lord than to put confidence in [flesh].

JOHN: It is better to take refuge in the Lord than to put confidence in princes.

[Psalm 118:1-9]

JESUS: I thank You that You have answered me and become my salvation. The stone which the builders rejected has become the head of the corner.

ALL: This is the Lord's doing; it is marvelous in our eyes. This is the day which the Lord has made. Let us rejoice and be glad in it. *[Psalm 118:21-24]*

(They blow out the candles and leave by the light of a taper.)

The Last Meal

TIME: The night before the crucifixion of Jesus

PLACE: A room with a table in the center. On it are a jug of wine, a goblet, a loaf of bread, a tray of herbs, and candles. Nearby a towel is draped over a stool beside a basin of water.

CHARACTERS: Judas
                  Peter
                  James
                  John
                  Jesus

(Onto a darkened stage a man gropes with a taper in hand. Four others follow. The first lights the candles.)

JUDAS: Very pleasant, Peter. You've done a good job.

PETER: John should share the credit.

JAMES: We're fortunate to get such a spacious room.

JOHN: Especially at Passover.

JUDAS: Who owns the room?

JOHN: A friend of Jesus.

JUDAS: A follower?

PETER: A sympathizer.

JUDAS: *(with a sneer)* Another hidden disciple!

JOHN: Don't be too harsh, Judas.

JUDAS: No? If we were more decisive I'm sure many more would join us openly. Instead we seem to be losing strength.

JAMES: You forget the entry into Jerusalem.

PETER: That was some show!

JUDAS: People are fickle. Up one day . . . down the next. If we don't make a move soon we won't hold them.

JAMES: Perhaps you're right Judas. *(turning to Jesus)* Master, isn't it time to establish the kingdom?

JESUS: The kingdom of God is being established.

JUDAS: But when do we make our move? When do we take power?

JESUS: I'm afraid you still misunderstand me.

PETER: Judas, you're too worried about finances. Even if we must struggle some more, I'm with the Master all the way.

JOHN: But Judas has a point. We can't go on like this much longer.

PETER: Like what?

JOHN: Teaching and healing, traveling around . . .

JUDAS: Without making a move to challenge the power structure.

PETER: But how, Judas? How?

JUDAS: You know my position.

JOHN: Armed rebellion isn't feasible. We aren't strong enough.

JUDAS: We won't get any stronger if we continue to lose support. Make a move and people will rise up . . . the way they did last Sunday.

JESUS: Power! Power! That's all you think about. I've so wanted to celebrate this Passover with you, and all you can talk about is power.

JUDAS: Evasion! . . . always evasion!

PETER: That's enough, Judas.

JOHN: No, Judas is right. We need to discuss the matter. We need a provisional government.

JUDAS: With James and John at the top, I suppose.

JAMES: I can think of no two better.

JUDAS: Just because your father's a prosperous fisherman.

JOHN: A little more business sense might not hurt you.

JUDAS: Are you insinuating I'm not honest.

JOHN: No. Just a little inefficient.

JUDAS: I'd like to see you balance the budget with dropping support.

JAMES: I'd start by cutting our givings to the poor.

JUDAS: And spend it on costly ointment?

PETER: We've been over that before.

JUDAS: He started it. I don't want two loudmouths in charge.

JAMES: Class! Social class is what we offer!

PETER: Class. That's a joke. Just because Zebedee did well at fishing, you think you own Galilee.

JAMES: At least we're better fishermen. That should count for something in this motly crew.

JESUS: Would you all listen a moment?

JUDAS: *(with a sneer)* Another lecture?

JESUS: On power. How many times have I insisted that the kingdom won't be established by lording it over one another.

JOHN: But someone must be in charge.

PETER: As long as it isn't you or James!

JUDAS: I agree that some decisive leadership is needed.

PETER: And you don't think Jesus has it?

JUDAS: He could be more decisive.

JOHN: I'm not complaining about the Master's leadership. But he needs some help. Someone should be second-in-command.

JESUS: *(He goes over, picks up a basin and pours some water into it.)* What do I have here?

PETER: A basin.

JAMES: Filled with water.

JESUS: And what is it for?

JOHN: Washing dusty feet.

JESUS: Precisely. *(Going over to Peter, He prepares to take off his sandals.)*

PETER: Oh no, Master, not me. You're not my servant. I can wash my own feet.

JESUS: You won't allow this courtesy?

PETER: It's not that. I should be doing it for **you**.

JESUS: Why?

PETER: Because you're the leader.

JESUS: And what does it mean if I the leader want to wash your feet?

PETER: I don't understand.

JUDAS: *(with a sneer)* This is true greatness . . . the ability to serve one another.

JESUS: Yes, Judas. But why the sneer? I don't feel I lose my dignity in this act. I express my love. If Peter won't let me wash his feet, he can't understand me.

PETER: I'm sorry, Master. If that's the way you feel, you can wash all of me.

JESUS: That's not necessary. It's the attitude, not the act.

JUDAS: So the kingdom will come as everyone goes around washing feet. If the army can't fight, at least it will have clean feet.

(There is an awkward silence. The disciples glare at Judas as if his sarcasm has gone too far.)

JESUS: I think it's time to eat. *(They take their places with Jesus in the center; Peter on his immediate right; Judas on the far right; John on the immediate left of Jesus and James on the far left, all facing the audience. If a note of realism is desired the participants could recline in white robes on cushions around a low table. Jesus pours wine into a goblet.)* Praise to You, our God, for creating the fruit of the vine. Take this and share it. *(The goblet is passed around; then a tray of herbs.)*

JAMES: Why is this night different from all other nights?

JESUS: It is the sacrifice of the Lord's Passover for he passed over the houses of the people of Israel in Egypt when he slew the Egyptians.

PETER: Praise the Lord!

JOHN: God be praised!

JUDAS: Praise the name of the Lord!

JAMES: Blessed be the name of the Lord from this time forth and for evermore!

PETER: From the rising of the sun to its setting the name of the Lord is to be praised!

JOHN: The Lord is high above all nations, and his glory above the heavens!

JUDAS: Who is like the Lord our God, who is seated on high, who looks far down upon the heavens and the earth?

JAMES: He raises the poor from the dust, and lifts the needy from the ash heap, to make them sit with princes.

ALL: Praise the Lord!   *[Psalm 113: 1-9]*

(Jesus pours a second goblet of wine and passes it around. Then he picks up a piece of bread.)

JESUS: This is the bread provided by God. It represents my body given up for your sake. Take and eat! *(They pass the bread around.)*

PETER: What do you mean saying your body given for us?

JESUS: I'm referring to my coming sufferings.

JAMES: What sufferings?

JESUS: The sufferings I've spoken of for the last several weeks. The true servant of God must suffer many things.

PETER: Don't worry. We'll protect you.

JESUS: From whom?

PETER: Your enemies, of course?

JESUS: And who will protect me from you?

JOHN: From us?

JESUS: Yes. I will be betrayed by one of you.

JAMES: Impossible. None of us would do such a thing. *(They all join in a chorus of denial.)*

JESUS: *(as Judas reaches over to tray of herbs)* The hardest blow is to be betrayed by someone who dips his hand into the same bowl. *(Judas pauses for an instant and then continues.)*

PETER: If everyone else forsakes you, I'll remain faithful . . . even to death.

JESUS: Peter, Satan will sift you like flour. Before the cock heralds the coming day you will deny me more than once.

PETER: Never!

JESUS: I pray that God will sustain you.

JOHN: We've had our differences and sometimes grown impatient but none of us would deny you. We believe you **will** establish God's kingdom.

JESUS: You don't seem to understand how the kingdom will be established.

PETER: We're willing to wait.

JESUS: It's not a matter of time; it's a question of method. What would you say if I told you to go out and buy weapons.

JUDAS: No need. Here are two swords. *(He draws out two short swords. Peter takes one.)*

JESUS: You wouldn't sense any inconsistency?

JUDAS: Not at all. That's the only power Rome understands.

JOHN: There's no need for arms. God will overturn the Romans.

JUDAS: While we sit around and talk.

JAMES: With God all things are possible!

JUDAS: But not probable.

JESUS: The kingdom is closer than you imagine. *(He pours out another goblet of wine.)* This wine represents my life's blood poured out for you in covenant. *(The goblet is passed around.)* I shall not drink again of the fruit of the vine until that day when I drink it new in the kingdom of God.

PETER: *(with surprise)* That soon?

JESUS: That soon!

JAMES: That's what we've been waiting for. *(He stands.)* This calls for a celebration!

PETER: *(also standing)* Let's join in the closing Psalm.

JESUS: O give thanks to the Lord, for he is good.

ALL: His steadfast love endures forever!

PETER: Let Israel say, "His steadfast love endures for ever."

JAMES: Let the house of Aaron say, "His steadfast love endures for ever."

JOHN: Let those who fear the Lord say, "His steadfast love endures for ever."

JESUS: Out of my distress I called on the Lord; the Lord answered me and set me free.

PETER: With the Lord on my side I do not fear. What can [people] do to me?

JUDAS: The Lord is on my side to help me; I shall look in triumph on those who hate me.

JAMES: It is better to take refuge in the Lord than to put confidence in [flesh].

JOHN: It is better to take refuge in the Lord than to put confidence in princes.

[Psalm 118:1-9]

JESUS: I thank You that You have answered me and become my salvation. The stone which the builders rejected has become the head of the corner.

ALL: This is the Lord's doing; it is marvelous in our eyes. This is the day which the Lord has made. Let us rejoice and be glad in it. *[Psalm 118:21-24]*

(They blow out the candles and leave by the light of a taper.)

The Last Word

TIME: The Day of crucifixion

PLACE: At the foot of the cross

CHARACTERS: Caius: a soldier, the cynic
Crispus: a soldier, in search
Marius: a soldier, rough and crude
Officer in charge
An off-stage voice

(Three soldiers huddle watching the outcome of the dice. A fourth stands to one side and slightly back from the edge of the chancel looking back at an upright cross.)

CAIUS: The tunic's mine.

CRISPUS: What luck!

MARIUS: The fruit of a misspent youth!

CAIUS: Obviously the gods know who is most deserving.

MARIUS: Then I've lost faith in the gods.

CRISPUS: You're not the only one.

MARIUS: You too, Crispus.

CRISPUS: No, Marius, I was thinking of him. *(pointing up to cross)*

MARIUS: Oh, the Galilean. Yeh, he's had quite a letdown.

CAIUS: I'd call it an uplift. *(He laughs.)*

MARIUS: These rebels should know not to challenge Rome.

CRISPUS: This one seemed different.

CAIUS: He's not the first to crack.

CRISPUS: That's not what I meant.

CAIUS: So, it's a deathbed conversion.

CRISPUS: Including forgiveness of his executioners?

MARIUS: Some of them go a bit crazy.

CAIUS: The intellectuals are the worst of the lot. It's usually the little guy who gets caught. This time it's one of the ringleaders.

CRISPUS: He was hardly that.

CAIUS: How stupid can you be, Crispus. Look at that crowd. Why would they be so angry if he hadn't caused trouble?

CRISPUS: You know damn well some people enjoy blood and guts.

VOICE: TRULY, I SAY TO YOU, TODAY YOU WILL BE WITH ME IN PARADISE.

[Luke 23:43]

MARIUS: It had something to do with religion. These people are crazy about religion.

CAIUS: Right! And no god is worth dying for!

CRISPUS: Is any god worth killing for?

CAIUS: You keep this up, Crispus, and you'll end up doing duty in Britain. We just do our job. If this guy didn't have the sense to keep out of trouble, is it our fault?

MARIUS: You should be used to these crucifixions by now.

CRISPUS: When it's a wild revolutionary or a hardened criminal, it's not so bad. Bu· when they nail up innocent people, something's wrong.

MARIUS: I'd keep that kind of talk to myself if I were you. You never know who's listening.

CAIUS: What makes you think he's so innocent?

CRISPUS: I heard him.

MARIUS: And caught religion!

CAIUS: What'd he say?

CRISPUS: Do you remember that young kid we caught in the Zealot skirmish three or four years ago?

MARIUS: Down below Jericho?

CRISPUS: Yes. After the slaughter we found him hiding in a cave, scared silly.

CAIUS: And we let him go with a warning?

VOICE: I THIRST. [*John 19:28*]

OFFICER: Marius, get some wine for the Galilean.

MARIUS: Yes, sir.

CRISPUS: *(in a low voice)* The old man seems a bit upset.

CAIUS: You'd think he'd be pretty tough by now. *(Marius puts a sponge on the end of a long pole and holds it up in the direction of the cross, lowers it and comes back to the group.)* What were you saying about the kid?

CRISPUS: Several months ago I spotted him.

MARIUS: Where?

CRISPUS: Following the Galilean.

CAIUS: What'd I tell you. No wonder the authorities were worried.

CRISPUS: I happened to be out of uniform at the time, and so I followed him and found myself at one of their outdoor meetings.

CAIUS: You didn't expect them to plot treason in public, did you?

CRISPUS: It wouldn't be the first time in this country. Remember that fellow who preached in the Jordan Valley?

CAIUS: John?

CRISPUS: The baptizer. He didn't pull his punches in public.

MARIUS: And look what it got him. Served up for Salome.

CRISPUS: The Galilean had a knack of telling stories and getting people to discuss them. He talked about a coming kingdom of God or heaven.

CAIUS: In public?

CRISPUS: Yes. And when he did I saw the eyes of our young friend light up. Some of the crowd asked when the kingdom was coming. Some even called him to start a rebellion on the spot. For a few moments I thought they were going to mob him and make him king. But he managed to stop them. Then he told them he wasn't talking about a political or military kingdom. He was talking about a new way of life God would make possible.

CAIUS: He probably spotted some spies in the crowd and knew they'd report him. I bet he was cooking up something.

CRISPUS: If he were, he missed his golden chance. More than half the crowd wandered off in disgust.

CAIUS: Including your friend?

CRISPUS: No. He stayed. But he looked very discouraged.

MARIUS: I knew we should have finished off that kid. Once a crummy Zealot, always a Zealot.

CRISPUS: You may be right about the kid, Marius. But I don't think the Galilean was planning rebellion.

CAIUS: Well, he must have lit a fire of some kind.

MARIUS: Just knocking about with young punks like that would be enough.

CAIUS: Forget the kid. Did the Galilean criticize Pilate or Caesar or Herod?

CRISPUS: Would that make him a revolutionary?

CAIUS: In this god-forsaken land, yes!

MARIUS: Especially in the company of riff-raff like that kid.

CRISPUS: Knock it off, Marius. I suppose you never got into trouble as a kid?

MARIUS: *(making a move as if to push Crispus)* Listen here.

CAIUS: *(holding him back)* Simmer down. *(then turning to Crispus)* You didn't answer my question. Did he criticize the authorities?

CRISPUS: Yes and no.

CAIUS: What kind of an answer is that?

CRISPUS: He had strong words for the religious leaders . . . the scribes and Pharisees.

CAIUS: I figured something must have annoyed them.

CRISPUS: But he didn't place all the blame on the leaders; he wanted everyone to repent.

MARIUS: No wonder he lost his followers.

CAIUS: To call for the overthrow of religion in this country is a dangerous business.

CRISPUS: It wasn't a call for the overthrow of religion. He wanted a renewal of religious life.

VOICE: ELOI, ELOI, LAMA SABACHTHANI! [*Mark 15:34*]

MARIUS: Good god, what was that?

CRISPUS: Local dialect!

CAIUS: Who is Eloi?

CRISPUS: Maybe Elijah, one of their prophets.

MARIUS: He'll need more than Elijah.

CAIUS: This is where religious renewal gets you. Those priests have a closed shop. You play the game their way or suffer the consequences.

CRISPUS: Maybe.

CAIUS: You expect some miraculous rescue? He's had it! And all his silly hopes.

CRISPUS: Perhaps.

CAIUS: Perhaps? Maybe? You're a fool, Crispus. That cross has been the end of many high-minded men. The only thing that matters in this world is power. If you haven't got that, be careful!

CRISPUS: You're a cynic, Caius. Is that how you live?

CAIUS: Come again?

CRISPUS: Is that how you treat your girlfriend?

CAIUS: Huh?

CRISPUS: By beating her into submission?

CAIUS: I'm talking about political matters.

CRISPUS: Maybe a little more compassion in politics wouldn't hurt.

CAIUS: Only the strong person can afford to be compassionate. If you're weak, people walk all over you.

CRISPUS: I'm not saying power is wrong; only that it can be misused.

CAIUS: *(pointing up)* And what did he have to say?

CRISPUS: That we should treat others with forgiveness, love, trust.

CAIUS: And look where it got him, Crispus. These people are too naive. Is that how you want to end?

VOICE: FATHER, INTO YOUR HANDS I COMMIT MY SPIRIT!   *[Luke 23:46]*

(The soldiers pause and look up.)

OFFICER: Your spear, Marius.

MARIUS: Yes, sir. *(He goes and thrusts his spear with force in the direction of the cross.)*

CAIUS: Is that how you want to end?

CRISPUS: Somehow it doesn't seem the end.

CAIUS: Are you trying to say he isn't dead?

CRISPUS: No. He's dead alright. But yet death doesn't seem the end.

CAIUS: You need a vacation, Crispus.

CRISPUS: I know it may sound strange, Caius. But somehow in his presence death — even this cruel death — seems different. It isn't a defeat. It's almost a victory, a triumphant shout that he is greater than all the power of evil.

CAIUS: You always were too sentimental, Crispus. For my money we've heard the last word from the Galilean.

The Last Word

TIME: The Day of crucifixion
PLACE: At the foot of the cross
CHARACTERS: Caius: a soldier, the cynic
                Crispus: a soldier, in search
                Marius: a soldier, rough and crude
                Officer in charge
                An off-stage voice

(Three soldiers huddle watching the outcome of the dice. A fourth stands to one side and slightly back from the edge of the chancel looking back at an upright cross.)

CAIUS: The tunic's mine.

CRISPUS: What luck!

MARIUS: The fruit of a misspent youth!

CAIUS: Obviously the gods know who is most deserving.

MARIUS: Then I've lost faith in the gods.

CRISPUS: You're not the only one.

MARIUS: You too, Crispus.

CRISPUS: No, Marius, I was thinking of him. *(pointing up to cross)*

MARIUS: Oh, the Galilean. Yeh, he's had quite a letdown.

CAIUS: I'd call it an uplift. *(He laughs.)*

MARIUS: These rebels should know not to challenge Rome.

CRISPUS: This one seemed different.

CAIUS: He's not the first to crack.

CRISPUS: That's not what I meant.

CAIUS: So, it's a deathbed conversion.

CRISPUS: Including forgiveness of his executioners?

MARIUS: Some of them go a bit crazy.

CAIUS: The intellectuals are the worst of the lot. It's usually the little guy who gets caught. This time it's one of the ringleaders.

CRISPUS: He was hardly that.

CAIUS: How stupid can you be, Crispus. Look at that crowd. Why would they be so angry if he hadn't caused trouble?

CRISPUS: You know damn well some people enjoy blood and guts.

VOICE: TRULY, I SAY TO YOU, TODAY YOU WILL BE WITH ME IN PARADISE.
                                                              [*Luke 23:43*]

MARIUS: It had something to do with religion. These people are crazy about religion.

CAIUS: Right! And no god is worth dying for!

CRISPUS: Is any god worth killing for?

CAIUS: You keep this up, Crispus, and you'll end up doing duty in Britain. We just do our job. If this guy didn't have the sense to keep out of trouble, is it our fault?

MARIUS: You should be used to these crucifixions by now.

CRISPUS: When it's a wild revolutionary or a hardened criminal, it's not so bad. But when they nail up innocent people, something's wrong.

MARIUS: I'd keep that kind of talk to myself if I were you. You never know who's listening.

CAIUS: What makes you think he's so innocent?

CRISPUS: I heard him.

MARIUS: And caught religion!

CAIUS: What'd he say?

CRISPUS: Do you remember that young kid we caught in the Zealot skirmish three or four years ago?

MARIUS: Down below Jericho?

CRISPUS: Yes. After the slaughter we found him hiding in a cave, scared silly.

CAIUS: And we let him go with a warning?

VOICE: I THIRST. [*John 19:28*]

OFFICER: Marius, get some wine for the Galilean.

MARIUS: Yes, sir.

CRISPUS: *(in a low voice)* The old man seems a bit upset.

CAIUS: You'd think he'd be pretty tough by now. *(Marius puts a sponge on the end of a long pole and holds it up in the direction of the cross, lowers it and comes back to the group.)* What were you saying about the kid?

CRISPUS: Several months ago I spotted him.

MARIUS: Where?

CRISPUS: Following the Galilean.

CAIUS: What'd I tell you. No wonder the authorities were worried.

CRISPUS: I happened to be out of uniform at the time, and so I followed him and found myself at one of their outdoor meetings.

CAIUS: You didn't expect them to plot treason in public, did you?

CRISPUS: It wouldn't be the first time in this country. Remember that fellow who preached in the Jordan Valley?

CAIUS: John?

CRISPUS: The baptizer. He didn't pull his punches in public.

MARIUS: And look what it got him. Served up for Salome.

CRISPUS: The Galilean had a knack of telling stories and getting people to discuss them. He talked about a coming kingdom of God or heaven.

CAIUS: In public?

CRISPUS: Yes. And when he did I saw the eyes of our young friend light up. Some of the crowd asked when the kingdom was coming. Some even called him to start a rebellion on the spot. For a few moments I thought they were going to mob him and make him king. But he managed to stop them. Then he told them he wasn't talking about a political or military kingdom. He was talking about a new way of life God would make possible.

CAIUS: He probably spotted some spies in the crowd and knew they'd report him. I bet he was cooking up something.

CRISPUS: If he were, he missed his golden chance. More than half the crowd wandered off in disgust.

CAIUS: Including your friend?

CRISPUS: No. He stayed. But he looked very discouraged.

MARIUS: I knew we should have finished off that kid. Once a crummy Zealot, always a Zealot.

CRISPUS: You may be right about the kid, Marius. But I don't think the Galilean was planning rebellion.

CAIUS: Well, he must have lit a fire of some kind.

MARIUS: Just knocking about with young punks like that would be enough.

CAIUS: Forget the kid. Did the Galilean criticize Pilate or Caesar or Herod?

CRISPUS: Would that make him a revolutionary?

CAIUS: In this god-forsaken land, yes!

MARIUS: Especially in the company of riff-raff like that kid.

CRISPUS: Knock it off, Marius. I suppose you never got into trouble as a kid?

MARIUS: *(making a move as if to push Crispus)* Listen here.

CAIUS: *(holding him back)* Simmer down. *(then turning to Crispus)* You didn't answer my question. Did he criticize the authorities?

CRISPUS: Yes and no.

CAIUS: What kind of an answer is that?

CRISPUS: He had strong words for the religious leaders . . . the scribes and Pharisees.

CAIUS: I figured something must have annoyed them.

CRISPUS: But he didn't place all the blame on the leaders; he wanted everyone to repent.

MARIUS: No wonder he lost his followers.

CAIUS: To call for the overthrow of religion in this country is a dangerous business.

CRISPUS: It wasn't a call for the overthrow of religion. He wanted a renewal of religious life.

VOICE: ELOI, ELOI, LAMA SABACHTHANI! [*Mark 15:34*]

MARIUS: Good god, what was that?

CRISPUS: Local dialect!

CAIUS: Who is Eloi?

CRISPUS: Maybe Elijah, one of their prophets.

MARIUS: He'll need more than Elijah.

CAIUS: This is where religious renewal gets you. Those priests have a closed shop. You play the game their way or suffer the consequences.

CRISPUS: Maybe.

CAIUS: You expect some miraculous rescue? He's had it! And all his silly hopes.

CRISPUS: Perhaps.

CAIUS: Perhaps? Maybe? You're a fool, Crispus. That cross has been the end of many high-minded men. The only thing that matters in this world is power. If you haven't got that, be careful!

CRISPUS: You're a cynic, Caius. Is that how you live?

CAIUS: Come again?

CRISPUS: Is that how you treat your girlfriend?

CAIUS: Huh?

CRISPUS: By beating her into submission?

CAIUS: I'm talking about political matters.

CRISPUS: Maybe a little more compassion in politics wouldn't hurt.

CAIUS: Only the strong person can afford to be compassionate. If you're weak, people walk all over you.

CRISPUS: I'm not saying power is wrong; only that it can be misused.

CAIUS: *(pointing up)* And what did he have to say?

CRISPUS: That we should treat others with forgiveness, love, trust.

CAIUS: And look where it got him, Crispus. These people are too naive. Is that how you want to end?

VOICE: FATHER, INTO YOUR HANDS I COMMIT MY SPIRIT! [*Luke 23:46*]

(The soldiers pause and look up.)

OFFICER: Your spear, Marius.

MARIUS: Yes, sir. *(He goes and thrusts his spear with force in the direction of the cross.)*

CAIUS: Is that how you want to end?

CRISPUS: Somehow it doesn't seem the end.

CAIUS: Are you trying to say he isn't dead?

CRISPUS: No. He's dead alright. But yet death doesn't seem the end.

CAIUS: You need a vacation, Crispus.

CRISPUS: I know it may sound strange, Caius. But somehow in his presence death — even this cruel death — seems different. It isn't a defeat. It's almost a victory, a triumphant shout that he is greater than all the power of evil.

CAIUS: You always were too sentimental, Crispus. For my money we've heard the last word from the Galilean.

The Last Word

TIME: The Day of crucifixion
PLACE: At the foot of the cross
CHARACTERS: Caius: a soldier, the cynic
     Crispus: a soldier, in search
     Marius: a soldier, rough and crude
     Officer in charge
     An off-stage voice

(Three soldiers huddle watching the outcome of the dice. A fourth stands to one side and slightly back from the edge of the chancel looking back at an upright cross.)

CAIUS: The tunic's mine.

CRISPUS: What luck!

MARIUS: The fruit of a misspent youth!

CAIUS: Obviously the gods know who is most deserving.

MARIUS: Then I've lost faith in the gods.

CRISPUS: You're not the only one.

MARIUS: You too, Crispus.

CRISPUS: No, Marius, I was thinking of him. *(pointing up to cross)*

MARIUS: Oh, the Galilean. Yeh, he's had quite a letdown.

CAIUS: I'd call it an uplift. *(He laughs.)*

MARIUS: These rebels should know not to challenge Rome.

CRISPUS: This one seemed different.

CAIUS: He's not the first to crack.

CRISPUS: That's not what I meant.

CAIUS: So, it's a deathbed conversion.

CRISPUS: Including forgiveness of his executioners?

MARIUS: Some of them go a bit crazy.

CAIUS: The intellectuals are the worst of the lot. It's usually the little guy who gets caught. This time it's one of the ringleaders.

CRISPUS: He was hardly that.

CAIUS: How stupid can you be, Crispus. Look at that crowd. Why would they be so angry if he hadn't caused trouble?

CRISPUS: You know damn well some people enjoy blood and guts.

VOICE: TRULY, I SAY TO YOU, TODAY YOU WILL BE WITH ME IN PARADISE.
                   [Luke 23:43]

MARIUS: It had something to do with religion. These people are crazy about religion.

CAIUS: Right! And no god is worth dying for!

CRISPUS: Is any god worth killing for?

CAIUS: You keep this up, Crispus, and you'll end up doing duty in Britain. We just do our job. If this guy didn't have the sense to keep out of trouble, is it our fault?

MARIUS: You should be used to these crucifixions by now.

CRISPUS: When it's a wild revolutionary or a hardened criminal, it's not so bad. But when they nail up innocent people, something's wrong.

MARIUS: I'd keep that kind of talk to myself if I were you. You never know who's listening.

CAIUS: What makes you think he's so innocent?

CRISPUS: I heard him.

MARIUS: And caught religion!

CAIUS: What'd he say?

CRISPUS: Do you remember that young kid we caught in the Zealot skirmish three or four years ago?

MARIUS: Down below Jericho?

CRISPUS: Yes. After the slaughter we found him hiding in a cave, scared silly.

CAIUS: And we let him go with a warning?

VOICE: I THIRST.   [*John 19:28*]

OFFICER: Marius, get some wine for the Galilean.

MARIUS: Yes, sir.

CRISPUS: *(in a low voice)* The old man seems a bit upset.

CAIUS: You'd think he'd be pretty tough by now. *(Marius puts a sponge on the end of a long pole and holds it up in the direction of the cross, lowers it and comes back to the group.)* What were you saying about the kid?

CRISPUS: Several months ago I spotted him.

MARIUS: Where?

CRISPUS: Following the Galilean.

CAIUS: What'd I tell you. No wonder the authorities were worried.

CRISPUS: I happened to be out of uniform at the time, and so I followed him and found myself at one of their outdoor meetings.

CAIUS: You didn't expect them to plot treason in public, did you?

CRISPUS: It wouldn't be the first time in this country. Remember that fellow who preached in the Jordan Valley?

CAIUS: John?

CRISPUS: The baptizer. He didn't pull his punches in public.

MARIUS: And look what it got him. Served up for Salome.

CRISPUS: The Galilean had a knack of telling stories and getting people to discuss them. He talked about a coming kingdom of God or heaven.

CAIUS: In public?

CRISPUS: Yes. And when he did I saw the eyes of our young friend light up. Some of the crowd asked when the kingdom was coming. Some even called him to start a rebellion on the spot. For a few moments I thought they were going to mob him and make him king. But he managed to stop them. Then he told them he wasn't talking about a political or military kingdom. He was talking about a new way of life God would make possible.

CAIUS: He probably spotted some spies in the crowd and knew they'd report him. I bet he was cooking up something.

CRISPUS: If he were, he missed his golden chance. More than half the crowd wandered off in disgust.

CAIUS: Including your friend?

CRISPUS: No. He stayed. But he looked very discouraged.

MARIUS: I knew we should have finished off that kid. Once a crummy Zealot, always a Zealot.

CRISPUS: You may be right about the kid, Marius. But I don't think the Galilean was planning rebellion.

CAIUS: Well, he must have lit a fire of some kind.

MARIUS: Just knocking about with young punks like that would be enough.

CAIUS: Forget the kid. Did the Galilean criticize Pilate or Caesar or Herod?

CRISPUS: Would that make him a revolutionary?

CAIUS: In this god-forsaken land, yes!

MARIUS: Especially in the company of riff-raff like that kid.

CRISPUS: Knock it off, Marius. I suppose you never got into trouble as a kid?

MARIUS: *(making a move as if to push Crispus)* Listen here.

CAIUS: *(holding him back)* Simmer down. *(then turning to Crispus)* You didn't answer my question. Did he criticize the authorities?

CRISPUS: Yes and no.

CAIUS: What kind of an answer is that?

CRISPUS: He had strong words for the religious leaders . . . the scribes and Pharisees.

CAIUS: I figured something must have annoyed them.

CRISPUS: But he didn't place all the blame on the leaders; he wanted everyone to repent.

MARIUS: No wonder he lost his followers.

CAIUS: To call for the overthrow of religion in this country is a dangerous business.

CRISPUS: It wasn't a call for the overthrow of religion. He wanted a renewal of religious life.

VOICE: ELOI, ELOI, LAMA SABACHTHANI!   [*Mark 15:34*]

MARIUS: Good god, what was that?

CRISPUS: Local dialect!

CAIUS: Who is Eloi?

CRISPUS: Maybe Elijah, one of their prophets.

MARIUS: He'll need more than Elijah.

CAIUS: This is where religious renewal gets you. Those priests have a closed shop. You play the game their way or suffer the consequences.

CRISPUS: Maybe.

CAIUS: You expect some miraculous rescue? He's had it! And all his silly hopes.

CRISPUS: Perhaps.

CAIUS: Perhaps? Maybe? You're a fool, Crispus. That cross has been the end of many high-minded men. The only thing that matters in this world is power. If you haven't got that, be careful!

CRISPUS: You're a cynic, Caius. Is that how you live?

CAIUS: Come again?

CRISPUS: Is that how you treat your girlfriend?

CAIUS: Huh?

CRISPUS: By beating her into submission?

CAIUS: I'm talking about political matters.

CRISPUS: Maybe a little more compassion in politics wouldn't hurt.

CAIUS: Only the strong person can afford to be compassionate. If you're weak, people walk all over you.

CRISPUS: I'm not saying power is wrong; only that it can be misused.

CAIUS: *(pointing up)* And what did he have to say?

CRISPUS: That we should treat others with forgiveness, love, trust.

CAIUS: And look where it got him, Crispus. These people are too naive. Is that how you want to end?

VOICE: FATHER, INTO YOUR HANDS I COMMIT MY SPIRIT! [*Luke 23:46*]

(The soldiers pause and look up.)

OFFICER: Your spear, Marius.

MARIUS: Yes, sir. *(He goes and thrusts his spear with force in the direction of the cross.)*

CAIUS: Is that how you want to end?

CRISPUS: Somehow it doesn't seem the end.

CAIUS: Are you trying to say he isn't dead?

CRISPUS: No. He's dead alright. But yet death doesn't seem the end.

CAIUS: You need a vacation, Crispus.

CRISPUS: I know it may sound strange, Caius. But somehow in his presence death — even this cruel death — seems different. It isn't a defeat. It's almost a victory, a triumphant shout that he is greater than all the power of evil.

CAIUS: You always were too sentimental, Crispus. For my money we've heard the last word from the Galilean.

The Last Word

TIME: The Day of crucifixion

PLACE: At the foot of the cross

CHARACTERS: Caius: a soldier, the cynic
Crispus: a soldier, in search
Marius: a soldier, rough and crude
Officer in charge
An off-stage voice

(Three soldiers huddle watching the outcome of the dice. A fourth stands to one side and slightly back from the edge of the chancel looking back at an upright cross.)

CAIUS: The tunic's mine.

CRISPUS: What luck!

MARIUS: The fruit of a misspent youth!

CAIUS: Obviously the gods know who is most deserving.

MARIUS: Then I've lost faith in the gods.

CRISPUS: You're not the only one.

MARIUS: You too, Crispus.

CRISPUS: No, Marius, I was thinking of him. *(pointing up to cross)*

MARIUS: Oh, the Galilean. Yeh, he's had quite a letdown.

CAIUS: I'd call it an uplift. *(He laughs.)*

MARIUS: These rebels should know not to challenge Rome.

CRISPUS: This one seemed different.

CAIUS: He's not the first to crack.

CRISPUS: That's not what I meant.

CAIUS: So, it's a deathbed conversion.

CRISPUS: Including forgiveness of his executioners?

MARIUS: Some of them go a bit crazy.

CAIUS: The intellectuals are the worst of the lot. It's usually the little guy who gets caught. This time it's one of the ringleaders.

CRISPUS: He was hardly that.

CAIUS: How stupid can you be, Crispus. Look at that crowd. Why would they be so angry if he hadn't caused trouble?

CRISPUS: You know damn well some people enjoy blood and guts.

VOICE: TRULY, I SAY TO YOU, TODAY YOU WILL BE WITH ME IN PARADISE.

[*Luke 23:43*]

MARIUS: It had something to do with religion. These people are crazy about religion.

CAIUS: Right! And no god is worth dying for!

CRISPUS: Is any god worth killing for?

CAIUS: You keep this up, Crispus, and you'll end up doing duty in Britain. We just do our job. If this guy didn't have the sense to keep out of trouble, is it our fault?

MARIUS: You should be used to these crucifixions by now.

CRISPUS: When it's a wild revolutionary or a hardened criminal, it's not so bad. But when they nail up innocent people, something's wrong.

MARIUS: I'd keep that kind of talk to myself if I were you. You never know who's listening.

CAIUS: What makes you think he's so innocent?

CRISPUS: I heard him.

MARIUS: And caught religion!

CAIUS: What'd he say?

CRISPUS: Do you remember that young kid we caught in the Zealot skirmish three or four years ago?

MARIUS: Down below Jericho?

CRISPUS: Yes. After the slaughter we found him hiding in a cave, scared silly.

CAIUS: And we let him go with a warning?

VOICE: I THIRST. *[John 19:28]*

OFFICER: Marius, get some wine for the Galilean.

MARIUS: Yes, sir.

CRISPUS: *(in a low voice)* The old man seems a bit upset.

CAIUS: You'd think he'd be pretty tough by now. *(Marius puts a sponge on the end of a long pole and holds it up in the direction of the cross, lowers it and comes back to the group.)* What were you saying about the kid?

CRISPUS: Several months ago I spotted him.

MARIUS: Where?

CRISPUS: Following the Galilean.

CAIUS: What'd I tell you. No wonder the authorities were worried.

CRISPUS: I happened to be out of uniform at the time, and so I followed him and found myself at one of their outdoor meetings.

CAIUS: You didn't expect them to plot treason in public, did you?

CRISPUS: It wouldn't be the first time in this country. Remember that fellow who preached in the Jordan Valley?

CAIUS: John?

CRISPUS: The baptizer. He didn't pull his punches in public.

MARIUS: And look what it got him. Served up for Salome.

CRISPUS: The Galilean had a knack of telling stories and getting people to discuss them. He talked about a coming kingdom of God or heaven.

CAIUS: In public?

CRISPUS: Yes. And when he did I saw the eyes of our young friend light up. Some of the crowd asked when the kingdom was coming. Some even called him to start a rebellion on the spot. For a few moments I thought they were going to mob him and make him king. But he managed to stop them. Then he told them he wasn't talking about a political or military kingdom. He was talking about a new way of life God would make possible.

CAIUS: He probably spotted some spies in the crowd and knew they'd report him. I bet he was cooking up something.

CRISPUS: If he were, he missed his golden chance. More than half the crowd wandered off in disgust.

CAIUS: Including your friend?

CRISPUS: No. He stayed. But he looked very discouraged.

MARIUS: I knew we should have finished off that kid. Once a crummy Zealot, always a Zealot.

CRISPUS: You may be right about the kid, Marius. But I don't think the Galilean was planning rebellion.

CAIUS: Well, he must have lit a fire of some kind.

MARIUS: Just knocking about with young punks like that would be enough.

CAIUS: Forget the kid. Did the Galilean criticize Pilate or Caesar or Herod?

CRISPUS: Would that make him a revolutionary?

CAIUS: In this god-forsaken land, yes!

MARIUS: Especially in the company of riff-raff like that kid.

CRISPUS: Knock it off, Marius. I suppose you never got into trouble as a kid?

MARIUS: *(making a move as if to push Crispus)* Listen here.

CAIUS: *(holding him back)* Simmer down. *(then turning to Crispus)* You didn't answer my question. Did he criticize the authorities?

CRISPUS: Yes and no.

CAIUS: What kind of an answer is that?

CRISPUS: He had strong words for the religious leaders . . . the scribes and Pharisees.

CAIUS: I figured something must have annoyed them.

CRISPUS: But he didn't place all the blame on the leaders; he wanted everyone to repent.

MARIUS: No wonder he lost his followers.

CAIUS: To call for the overthrow of religion in this country is a dangerous business.

CRISPUS: It wasn't a call for the overthrow of religion. He wanted a renewal of religious life.

VOICE: ELOI, ELOI, LAMA SABACHTHANI!   [*Mark 15:34*]

MARIUS: Good god, what was that?

CRISPUS: Local dialect!

CAIUS: Who is Eloi?

CRISPUS: Maybe Elijah, one of their prophets.

MARIUS: He'll need more than Elijah.

CAIUS: This is where religious renewal gets you. Those priests have a closed shop. You play the game their way or suffer the consequences.

CRISPUS: Maybe.

CAIUS: You expect some miraculous rescue? He's had it! And all his silly hopes.

CRISPUS: Perhaps.

CAIUS: Perhaps? Maybe? You're a fool, Crispus. That cross has been the end of many high-minded men. The only thing that matters in this world is power. If you haven't got that, be careful!

CRISPUS: You're a cynic, Caius. Is that how you live?

CAIUS: Come again?

CRISPUS: Is that how you treat your girlfriend?

CAIUS: Huh?

CRISPUS: By beating her into submission?

CAIUS: I'm talking about political matters.

CRISPUS: Maybe a little more compassion in politics wouldn't hurt.

CAIUS: Only the strong person can afford to be compassionate. If you're weak, people walk all over you.

CRISPUS: I'm not saying power is wrong; only that it can be misused.

CAIUS: *(pointing up)* And what did he have to say?

CRISPUS: That we should treat others with forgiveness, love, trust.

CAIUS: And look where it got him, Crispus. These people are too naive. Is that how you want to end?

VOICE: FATHER, INTO YOUR HANDS I COMMIT MY SPIRIT! [*Luke 23:46*]

(The soldiers pause and look up.)

OFFICER: Your spear, Marius.

MARIUS: Yes, sir. *(He goes and thrusts his spear with force in the direction of the cross.)*

CAIUS: Is that how you want to end?

CRISPUS: Somehow it doesn't seem the end.

CAIUS: Are you trying to say he isn't dead?

CRISPUS: No. He's dead alright. But yet death doesn't seem the end.

CAIUS: You need a vacation, Crispus.

CRISPUS: I know it may sound strange, Caius. But somehow in his presence death — even this cruel death — seems different. It isn't a defeat. It's almost a victory, a triumphant shout that he is greater than all the power of evil.

CAIUS: You always were too sentimental, Crispus. For my money we've heard the last word from the Galilean.

The Last Word

TIME: The Day of crucifixion

PLACE: At the foot of the cross

CHARACTERS: Caius: a soldier, the cynic
Crispus: a soldier, in search
Marius: a soldier, rough and crude
Officer in charge
An off-stage voice

(Three soldiers huddle watching the outcome of the dice. A fourth stands to one side and slightly back from the edge of the chancel looking back at an upright cross.)

CAIUS: The tunic's mine.

CRISPUS: What luck!

MARIUS: The fruit of a misspent youth!

CAIUS: Obviously the gods know who is most deserving.

MARIUS: Then I've lost faith in the gods.

CRISPUS: You're not the only one.

MARIUS: You too, Crispus.

CRISPUS: No, Marius, I was thinking of him. *(pointing up to cross)*

MARIUS: Oh, the Galilean. Yeh, he's had quite a letdown.

CAIUS: I'd call it an uplift. *(He laughs.)*

MARIUS: These rebels should know not to challenge Rome.

CRISPUS: This one seemed different.

CAIUS: He's not the first to crack.

CRISPUS: That's not what I meant.

CAIUS: So, it's a deathbed conversion.

CRISPUS: Including forgiveness of his executioners?

MARIUS: Some of them go a bit crazy.

CAIUS: The intellectuals are the worst of the lot. It's usually the little guy who gets caught. This time it's one of the ringleaders.

CRISPUS: He was hardly that.

CAIUS: How stupid can you be, Crispus. Look at that crowd. Why would they be so angry if he hadn't caused trouble?

CRISPUS: You know damn well some people enjoy blood and guts.

VOICE: TRULY, I SAY TO YOU, TODAY YOU WILL BE WITH ME IN PARADISE.

[*Luke 23:43*]

MARIUS: It had something to do with religion. These people are crazy about religion.

CAIUS: Right! And no god is worth dying for!

CRISPUS: Is any god worth killing for?

CAIUS: You keep this up, Crispus, and you'll end up doing duty in Britain. We just do our job. If this guy didn't have the sense to keep out of trouble, is it our fault?

MARIUS: You should be used to these crucifixions by now.

CRISPUS: When it's a wild revolutionary or a hardened criminal, it's not so bad. But when they nail up innocent people, something's wrong.

MARIUS: I'd keep that kind of talk to myself if I were you. You never know who's listening.

CAIUS: What makes you think he's so innocent?

CRISPUS: I heard him.

MARIUS: And caught religion!

CAIUS: What'd he say?

CRISPUS: Do you remember that young kid we caught in the Zealot skirmish three or four years ago?

MARIUS: Down below Jericho?

CRISPUS: Yes. After the slaughter we found him hiding in a cave, scared silly.

CAIUS: And we let him go with a warning?

VOICE: I THIRST. [*John 19:28*]

OFFICER: Marius, get some wine for the Galilean.

MARIUS: Yes, sir.

CRISPUS: *(in a low voice)* The old man seems a bit upset.

CAIUS: You'd think he'd be pretty tough by now. *(Marius puts a sponge on the end of a long pole and holds it up in the direction of the cross, lowers it and comes back to the group.)* What were you saying about the kid?

CRISPUS: Several months ago I spotted him.

MARIUS: Where?

CRISPUS: Following the Galilean.

CAIUS: What'd I tell you. No wonder the authorities were worried.

CRISPUS: I happened to be out of uniform at the time, and so I followed him and found myself at one of their outdoor meetings.

CAIUS: You didn't expect them to plot treason in public, did you?

CRISPUS: It wouldn't be the first time in this country. Remember that fellow who preached in the Jordan Valley?

CAIUS: John?

CRISPUS: The baptizer. He didn't pull his punches in public.

MARIUS: And look what it got him. Served up for Salome.

CRISPUS: The Galilean had a knack of telling stories and getting people to discuss them. He talked about a coming kingdom of God or heaven.

CAIUS: In public?

CRISPUS: Yes. And when he did I saw the eyes of our young friend light up. Some of the crowd asked when the kingdom was coming. Some even called him to start a rebellion on the spot. For a few moments I thought they were going to mob him and make him king. But he managed to stop them. Then he told them he wasn't talking about a political or military kingdom. He was talking about a new way of life God would make possible.

CAIUS: He probably spotted some spies in the crowd and knew they'd report him. I bet he was cooking up something.

CRISPUS: If he were, he missed his golden chance. More than half the crowd wandered off in disgust.

CAIUS: Including your friend?

CRISPUS: No. He stayed. But he looked very discouraged.

MARIUS: I knew we should have finished off that kid. Once a crummy Zealot, always a Zealot.

CRISPUS: You may be right about the kid, Marius. But I don't think the Galilean was planning rebellion.

CAIUS: Well, he must have lit a fire of some kind.

MARIUS: Just knocking about with young punks like that would be enough.

CAIUS: Forget the kid. Did the Galilean criticize Pilate or Caesar or Herod?

CRISPUS: Would that make him a revolutionary?

CAIUS: In this god-forsaken land, yes!

MARIUS: Especially in the company of riff-raff like that kid.

CRISPUS: Knock it off, Marius. I suppose you never got into trouble as a kid?

MARIUS: *(making a move as if to push Crispus)* Listen here.

CAIUS: *(holding him back)* Simmer down. *(then turning to Crispus)* You didn't answer my question. Did he criticize the authorities?

CRISPUS: Yes and no.

CAIUS: What kind of an answer is that?

CRISPUS: He had strong words for the religious leaders . . . the scribes and Pharisees.

CAIUS: I figured something must have annoyed them.

CRISPUS: But he didn't place all the blame on the leaders; he wanted everyone to repent.

MARIUS: No wonder he lost his followers.

CAIUS: To call for the overthrow of religion in this country is a dangerous business.

CRISPUS: It wasn't a call for the overthrow of religion. He wanted a renewal of religious life.

VOICE: ELOI, ELOI, LAMA SABACHTHANI! [*Mark 15:34*]

MARIUS: Good god, what was that?

CRISPUS: Local dialect!

CAIUS: Who is Eloi?

CRISPUS: Maybe Elijah, one of their prophets.

MARIUS: He'll need more than Elijah.

CAIUS: This is where religious renewal gets you. Those priests have a closed shop. You play the game their way or suffer the consequences.

CRISPUS: Maybe.

CAIUS: You expect some miraculous rescue? He's had it! And all his silly hopes.

CRISPUS: Perhaps.

CAIUS: Perhaps? Maybe? You're a fool, Crispus. That cross has been the end of many high-minded men. The only thing that matters in this world is power. If you haven't got that, be careful!

CRISPUS: You're a cynic, Caius. Is that how you live?

CAIUS: Come again?

CRISPUS: Is that how you treat your girlfriend?

CAIUS: Huh?

CRISPUS: By beating her into submission?

CAIUS: I'm talking about political matters.

CRISPUS: Maybe a little more compassion in politics wouldn't hurt.

CAIUS: Only the strong person can afford to be compassionate. If you're weak, people walk all over you.

CRISPUS: I'm not saying power is wrong; only that it can be misused.

CAIUS: *(pointing up)* And what did he have to say?

CRISPUS: That we should treat others with forgiveness, love, trust.

CAIUS: And look where it got him, Crispus. These people are too naive. Is that how you want to end?

VOICE: FATHER, INTO YOUR HANDS I COMMIT MY SPIRIT! [*Luke 23:46*]

(The soldiers pause and look up.)

OFFICER: Your spear, Marius.

MARIUS: Yes, sir. *(He goes and thrusts his spear with force in the direction of the cross.)*

CAIUS: Is that how you want to end?

CRISPUS: Somehow it doesn't seem the end.

CAIUS: Are you trying to say he isn't dead?

CRISPUS: No. He's dead alright. But yet death doesn't seem the end.

CAIUS: You need a vacation, Crispus.

CRISPUS: I know it may sound strange, Caius. But somehow in his presence death — even this cruel death — seems different. It isn't a defeat. It's almost a victory, a triumphant shout that he is greater than all the power of evil.

CAIUS: You always were too sentimental, Crispus. For my money we've heard the last word from the Galilean.

A Strange Meeting

TIME: Easter Sunday afternoon

PLACE: An inn on the road from Jerusalem to Emmaus

CHARACTERS: Cleopas
Anna: his wife
A Stranger
A Waiter

(Cleopas and Anna are seated at a table for four.)

STRANGER: Do you mind if I sit down?

CLEOPAS: Not at all.

STRANGER: The inn's crowded!

CLEOPAS: Yes. *(awkward pause)*

STRANGER: I hope I'm not intruding.

CLEOPAS: No. *(another pause)*

STRANGER: If you'd like to be alone, I can find another spot. *(He begins to rise.)*

CLEOPAS: Stay where you are, stranger. We were just talking over the events of the last few days.

STRANGER: You look dejected.

CLEOPAS: That's an understatement.

STRANGER: Anything I can do to help?

CLEOPAS: Not really.

STRANGER: Where are you from?

CLEOPAS: Galilee.

STRANGER: Up for the Passover?

CLEOPAS: Yes . . . and you?

STRANGER: On my way to Galilee.

ANNA: You were in Jerusalem for the Passover?

STRANGER: Yes.

ANNA: And you don't feel depressed?

STRANGER: About what?

ANNA: About what took place! . . . Those crucifixions!

STRANGER: Nothing new about crucifixions.

ANNA: You weren't disturbed?

STRANGER: I don't enjoy crucifixions, if that's what you mean.

ANNA: You didn't feel the death of Jesus was a great tragedy?

STRANGER: No system of justice is perfect.

CLEOPAS: You're a cool one.

STRANGER: You felt deeply about Jesus?

ANNA: We believed he was a prophet.

STRANGER: Israel's had many prophets.

ANNA: But few, if any, spoke and acted as he did.

STRANGER: Obviously he failed to persuade everyone.

ANNA: Only those blind to his message could refuse.

CLEOPAS: The religious leaders.

STRANGER: But what of the common people?

CLEOPAS: They were for him.

STRANGER: Who shouted for his crucifixion?

CLEOPAS: Mobs can be manipulated.

STRANGER: Yes. But how deep was their loyalty?

ANNA: If they had only known him better.

STRANGER: As you did?

ANNA: As we did.

STRANGER: Yet you feel the crucifixion ended everything?

CLEOPAS: A dead man can't do much.

ANNA: Particularly against Rome.

STRANGER: What did you expect him to do . . . when he was alive, that is?

CLEOPAS: He was going to liberate Israel.

STRANGER: In what way?

ANNA: It didn't matter to us.

CLEOPAS: Some believed it would be by military action . . . some kind of armed insurrection.

STRANGER: From what I've heard, he didn't seem interested in force.

CLEOPAS: He wasn't. And most of those who were looking for it left us long ago. But some thought he might be concealing his plans until the right moment.

ANNA: Others expected God to intervene in some miraculous way from above.

STRANGER: And what kind of kingdom did you expect?

ANNA: One in which there would be freedom to live and worship without oppression.

STRANGER: You're not free to worship and serve God?

CLEOPAS: With the Temple in the hands of traitors and hypocrites?

STRANGER: Yes. I understand he was critical of religious hypocrisy.

CLEOPAS: *(with glee)* You should have heard him . . . those blistering words against the scribes and Pharisees.

STRANGER: But I understand he also said, "Except your righteousness exceed the righteousness of the scribe and Pharisee you shall not see the kingdom of God"?

CLEOPAS: *(slowly and somewhat deflated)* Yes, I recall that one.

ANNA: He could be puzzling at times.

CLEOPAS: He would call us to live with moral integrity and then befriend the hated outcast.

ANNA: In order to bring them back to God, of course.

CLEOPAS: But still as if morality made no difference.

ANNA: He believed good and evil alike were loved by God.

CLEOPAS: Most puzzling.

STRANGER: Didn't he give you any warning that he might be put to death? No instruction of what you should do if that took place?

CLEOPAS: He did speak of suffering and death. But we thought that was just a warning that things might not be too easy.

ANNA: He was warned not to go to Jerusalem for this Passover.

STRANGER: He obviously refused.

ANNA: He was a very determined man. Loving and tender but determined.

STRANGER: Yet he's now a failure?

ANNA: I wouldn't put it that way. But our hopes were so high. God's kingdom seemed so certain.

STRANGER: And all that is now lost?

CLEOPAS: What can we do without a leader like him?

STRANGER: But surely he must have had a vision of something beyond his death.

CLEOPAS: He believed in the resurrection at the last day, if that's what you mean?

ANNA: There's even a rumor that he has already risen from the dead.

STRANGER: A rumor?

CLEOPAS: Some women went to the grave this morning and were unable to find the body. They returned with stories of angels and an empty tomb.

STRANGER: Did others investigate?

ANNA: Some of the disciples. But no one could find the body.

CLEOPAS: I'm sure someone stole it. Probably the authorities. They couldn't let him rest even in death . . . Ah, here's the waiter. Would you be our guest?

STRANGER: Thank you.

CLEOPAS: I'd recommend the fish.

STRANGER: Alright with me.

CLEOPAS: Three orders of the special.

WAITER: Yes, sir.

CLEOPAS: Now, where were we?

STRANGER: You were saying his body had been stolen.

CLEOPAS: Yes. That's my theory.

STRANGER: Is the body that important?

CLEOPAS: Without a body you can't be a person.

STRANGER: But isn't God able to raise up new life?

CLEOPAS: Without a body?

STRANGER: Without the same body.

CLEOPAS: To me a body is a body.

STRANGER: But do you so limit the power of God?

CLEOPAS: I can't think of life without a body.

STRANGER: But what about a transformed body? One you might not recognize?

CLEOPAS: What are you trying to say?

STRANGER: God is always bringing new life out of despair. The Scriptures are full of it. During the seige of Jerusalem, Jeremiah bought land to show there would be life after the seige. Ezekiel saw a valley of dry bones coming to new life.

CLEOPAS: But those promises applied to the nation.

ANNA: Individuals don't rise from the dead . . . except in the day of resurrection.

WAITER: Your meals. (*He sets down the three dishes of fish, three goblets, a loaf of bread, and a jug of wine.*)

CLEOPAS: Stranger, would you give thanks?

STRANGER: (*as he breaks the loaf*) This is life broken for us. (*as he pours wine into the goblets*) And this is a life poured out for us. And to God be all thanks.

CLEOPAS & ANNA: To God be all thanks.

ANNA: You believe his death was for some purpose?

STRANGER: God's true servant is often treated harshly. He is brought as a lamb to the slaughter. He is arrested and sentenced and led off to die. And no one cares about his fate.

ANNA: He certainly suffered.

CLEOPAS: But to what purpose? What improvement has it brought?

STRANGER: Has it not shown that love can conquer hate? That the power of God is greater than human evil.

CLEOPAS: I can't say it has. To me it seems so futile.

STRANGER: I can understand your feelings. But don't forget the presence and power of God. *(pause)* However I must be on my way. *(He rises.)*

CLEOPAS: So soon?

STRANGER: Yes. But thank you for your kind hospitality.

CLEOPAS: Perhaps we'll meet again.

STRANGER: We will. *(He leaves.)*

CLEOPAS: A strange person. We never did learn his name.

ANNA: Or where in Galilee he lived. But he was familiar for some reason.

CLEOPAS: He certainly knew the Scriptures.

ANNA: And spoke with such feeling. Didn't it impress you?

CLEOPAS: It reminded me of someone.

ANNA: I had the same feeling. You don't suppose . . .

CLEOPAS: He spoke of resurrection.

ANNA: And changed bodies.

CLEOPAS: And hope.

ANNA: And the power and presence of God.

CLEOPAS: Could it be . . . ?

ANNA: With God all things are possible.

CLEOPAS: *(with still a note of uncertainty)* It must be. We didn't recognize him . . . *(with growing certainty)* but it must be. The way he broke the bread and blessed the wine.

ANNA: It was! It was the risen Christ! Alive in our midst! In a stranger!

CLEOPAS: The women were right! We must share this news with the others . . . without delay. *(They rise and leave.)*

A Strange Meeting

TIME: Easter Sunday afternoon

PLACE: An inn on the road from Jerusalem to Emmaus

CHARACTERS: Cleopas
Anna: his wife
A Stranger
A Waiter

(Cleopas and Anna are seated at a table for four.)

STRANGER: Do you mind if I sit down?

CLEOPAS: Not at all.

STRANGER: The inn's crowded!

CLEOPAS: Yes. *(awkward pause)*

STRANGER: I hope I'm not intruding.

CLEOPAS: No. *(another pause)*

STRANGER: If you'd like to be alone, I can find another spot. *(He begins to rise.)*

CLEOPAS: Stay where you are, stranger. We were just talking over the events of the last few days.

STRANGER: You look dejected.

CLEOPAS: That's an understatement.

STRANGER: Anything I can do to help?

CLEOPAS: Not really.

STRANGER: Where are you from?

CLEOPAS: Galilee.

STRANGER: Up for the Passover?

CLEOPAS: Yes . . . and you?

STRANGER: On my way to Galilee.

ANNA: You were in Jerusalem for the Passover?

STRANGER: Yes.

ANNA: And you don't feel depressed?

STRANGER: About what?

ANNA: About what took place! . . . Those crucifixions!

STRANGER: Nothing new about crucifixions.

ANNA: You weren't disturbed?

STRANGER: I don't enjoy crucifixions, if that's what you mean.

ANNA: You didn't feel the death of Jesus was a great tragedy?

STRANGER: No system of justice is perfect.

CLEOPAS: You're a cool one.

STRANGER: You felt deeply about Jesus?

ANNA: We believed he was a prophet.

STRANGER: Israel's had many prophets.

ANNA: But few, if any, spoke and acted as he did.

STRANGER: Obviously he failed to persuade everyone.

ANNA: Only those blind to his message could refuse.

CLEOPAS: The religious leaders.

STRANGER: But what of the common people?

CLEOPAS: They were for him.

STRANGER: Who shouted for his crucifixion?

CLEOPAS: Mobs can be manipulated.

STRANGER: Yes. But how deep was their loyalty?

ANNA: If they had only known him better.

STRANGER: As you did?

ANNA: As we did.

STRANGER: Yet you feel the crucifixion ended everything?

CLEOPAS: A dead man can't do much.

ANNA: Particularly against Rome.

STRANGER: What did you expect him to do . . . when he was alive, that is?

CLEOPAS: He was going to liberate Israel.

STRANGER: In what way?

ANNA: It didn't matter to us.

CLEOPAS: Some believed it would be by military action . . . some kind of armed insurrection.

STRANGER: From what I've heard, he didn't seem interested in force.

CLEOPAS: He wasn't. And most of those who were looking for it left us long ago. But some thought he might be concealing his plans until the right moment.

ANNA: Others expected God to intervene in some miraculous way from above.

STRANGER: And what kind of kingdom did you expect?

ANNA: One in which there would be freedom to live and worship without oppression.

STRANGER: You're not free to worship and serve God?

CLEOPAS: With the Temple in the hands of traitors and hypocrites?

STRANGER: Yes. I understand he was critical of religious hypocrisy.

CLEOPAS: *(with glee)* You should have heard him . . . those blistering words against the scribes and Pharisees.

STRANGER: But I understand he also said, "Except your righteousness exceed the righteousness of the scribe and Pharisee you shall not see the kingdom of God"?

CLEOPAS: *(slowly and somewhat deflated)* Yes, I recall that one.

ANNA: He could be puzzling at times.

CLEOPAS: He would call us to live with moral integrity and then befriend the hated outcast.

ANNA: In order to bring them back to God, of course.

CLEOPAS: But still as if morality made no difference.

ANNA: He believed good and evil alike were loved by God.

CLEOPAS: Most puzzling.

STRANGER: Didn't he give you any warning that he might be put to death? No instruction of what you should do if that took place?

CLEOPAS: He did speak of suffering and death. But we thought that was just a warning that things might not be too easy.

ANNA: He was warned not to go to Jerusalem for this Passover.

STRANGER: He obviously refused.

ANNA: He was a very determined man. Loving and tender but determined.

STRANGER: Yet he's now a failure?

ANNA: I wouldn't put it that way. But our hopes were so high. God's kingdom seemed so certain.

STRANGER: And all that is now lost?

CLEOPAS: What can we do without a leader like him?

STRANGER: But surely he must have had a vision of something beyond his death.

CLEOPAS: He believed in the resurrection at the last day, if that's what you mean?

ANNA: There's even a rumor that he has already risen from the dead.

STRANGER: A rumor?

CLEOPAS: Some women went to the grave this morning and were unable to find the body. They returned with stories of angels and an empty tomb.

STRANGER: Did others investigate?

ANNA: Some of the disciples. But no one could find the body.

CLEOPAS: I'm sure someone stole it. Probably the authorities. They couldn't let him rest even in death . . . Ah, here's the waiter. Would you be our guest?

STRANGER: Thank you.

CLEOPAS: I'd recommend the fish.

STRANGER: Alright with me.

CLEOPAS: Three orders of the special.

WAITER: Yes, sir.

CLEOPAS: Now, where were we?

STRANGER: You were saying his body had been stolen.

CLEOPAS: Yes. That's my theory.

STRANGER: Is the body that important?

CLEOPAS: Without a body you can't be a person.

STRANGER: But isn't God able to raise up new life?

CLEOPAS: Without a body?

STRANGER: Without the same body.

CLEOPAS: To me a body is a body.

STRANGER: But do you so limit the power of God?

CLEOPAS: I can't think of life without a body.

STRANGER: But what about a transformed body? One you might not recognize?

CLEOPAS: What are you trying to say?

STRANGER: God is always bringing new life out of despair. The Scriptures are full of it. During the seige of Jerusalem, Jeremiah bought land to show there would be life after the seige. Ezekiel saw a valley of dry bones coming to new life.

CLEOPAS: But those promises applied to the nation.

ANNA: Individuals don't rise from the dead . . . except in the day of resurrection.

WAITER: Your meals. *(He sets down the three dishes of fish, three goblets, a loaf of bread, and a jug of wine.)*

CLEOPAS: Stranger, would you give thanks?

STRANGER: *(as he breaks the loaf)* This is life broken for us. *(as he pours wine into the goblets)* And this is a life poured out for us. And to God be all thanks.

CLEOPAS & ANNA: To God be all thanks.

ANNA: You believe his death was for some purpose?

STRANGER: God's true servant is often treated harshly. He is brought as a lamb to the slaughter. He is arrested and sentenced and led off to die. And no one cares about his fate.

ANNA: He certainly suffered.

CLEOPAS: But to what purpose? What improvement has it brought?

STRANGER: Has it not shown that love can conquer hate? That the power of God is greater than human evil.

CLEOPAS: I can't say it has. To me it seems so futile.

STRANGER: I can understand your feelings. But don't forget the presence and power of God. *(pause)* However I must be on my way. *(He rises.)*

CLEOPAS: So soon?

STRANGER: Yes. But thank you for your kind hospitality.

CLEOPAS: Perhaps we'll meet again.

STRANGER: We will. *(He leaves.)*

CLEOPAS: A strange person. We never did learn his name.

ANNA: Or where in Galilee he lived. But he was familiar for some reason.

CLEOPAS: He certainly knew the Scriptures.

ANNA: And spoke with such feeling. Didn't it impress you?

CLEOPAS: It reminded me of someone.

ANNA: I had the same feeling. You don't suppose . . .

CLEOPAS: He spoke of resurrection.

ANNA: And changed bodies.

CLEOPAS: And hope.

ANNA: And the power and presence of God.

CLEOPAS: Could it be . . . ?

ANNA: With God all things are possible.

CLEOPAS: *(with still a note of uncertainty)* It must be. We didn't recognize him . . . *(with growing certainty)* but it must be. The way he broke the bread and blessed the wine.

ANNA: It was! It was the risen Christ! Alive in our midst! In a stranger!

CLEOPAS: The women were right! We must share this news with the others . . . without delay. *(They rise and leave.)*

A Strange Meeting

TIME: Easter Sunday afternoon

PLACE: An inn on the road from Jerusalem to Emmaus

CHARACTERS: Cleopas
              Anna: his wife
              A Stranger
              A Waiter

(Cleopas and Anna are seated at a table for four.)

STRANGER: Do you mind if I sit down?

CLEOPAS: Not at all.

STRANGER: The inn's crowded!

CLEOPAS: Yes. *(awkward pause)*

STRANGER: I hope I'm not intruding.

CLEOPAS: No. *(another pause)*

STRANGER: If you'd like to be alone, I can find another spot. *(He begins to rise.)*

CLEOPAS: Stay where you are, stranger. We were just talking over the events of the last few days.

STRANGER: You look dejected.

CLEOPAS: That's an understatement.

STRANGER: Anything I can do to help?

CLEOPAS: Not really.

STRANGER: Where are you from?

CLEOPAS: Galilee.

STRANGER: Up for the Passover?

CLEOPAS: Yes . . . and you?

STRANGER: On my way to Galilee.

ANNA: You were in Jerusalem for the Passover?

STRANGER: Yes.

ANNA: And you don't feel depressed?

STRANGER: About what?

ANNA: About what took place! . . . Those crucifixions!

STRANGER: Nothing new about crucifixions.

ANNA: You weren't disturbed?

STRANGER: I don't enjoy crucifixions, if that's what you mean.

ANNA: You didn't feel the death of Jesus was a great tragedy?

STRANGER: No system of justice is perfect.

CLEOPAS: You're a cool one.

STRANGER: You felt deeply about Jesus?

ANNA: We believed he was a prophet.

STRANGER: Israel's had many prophets.

ANNA: But few, if any, spoke and acted as he did.

STRANGER: Obviously he failed to persuade everyone.

ANNA: Only those blind to his message could refuse.

CLEOPAS: The religious leaders.

STRANGER: But what of the common people?

CLEOPAS: They were for him.

STRANGER: Who shouted for his crucifixion?

CLEOPAS: Mobs can be manipulated.

STRANGER: Yes. But how deep was their loyalty?

ANNA: If they had only known him better.

STRANGER: As you did?

ANNA: As we did.

STRANGER: Yet you feel the crucifixion ended everything?

CLEOPAS: A dead man can't do much.

ANNA: Particularly against Rome.

STRANGER: What did you expect him to do . . . when he was alive, that is?

CLEOPAS: He was going to liberate Israel.

STRANGER: In what way?

ANNA: It didn't matter to us.

CLEOPAS: Some believed it would be by military action . . . some kind of armed insurrection.

STRANGER: From what I've heard, he didn't seem interested in force.

CLEOPAS: He wasn't. And most of those who were looking for it left us long ago. But some thought he might be concealing his plans until the right moment.

ANNA: Others expected God to intervene in some miraculous way from above.

STRANGER: And what kind of kingdom did you expect?

ANNA: One in which there would be freedom to live and worship without oppression.

STRANGER: You're not free to worship and serve God?

CLEOPAS: With the Temple in the hands of traitors and hypocrites?

STRANGER: Yes. I understand he was critical of religious hypocrisy.

CLEOPAS: *(with glee)* You should have heard him . . . those blistering words against the scribes and Pharisees.

STRANGER: But I understand he also said, "Except your righteousness exceed the righteousness of the scribe and Pharisee you shall not see the kingdom of God"?

CLEOPAS: *(slowly and somewhat deflated)* Yes, I recall that one.

ANNA: He could be puzzling at times.

CLEOPAS: He would call us to live with moral integrity and then befriend the hated outcast.

ANNA: In order to bring them back to God, of course.

CLEOPAS: But still as if morality made no difference.

ANNA: He believed good and evil alike were loved by God.

CLEOPAS: Most puzzling.

STRANGER: Didn't he give you any warning that he might be put to death? No instruction of what you should do if that took place?

CLEOPAS: He did speak of suffering and death. But we thought that was just a warning that things might not be too easy.

ANNA: He was warned not to go to Jerusalem for this Passover.

STRANGER: He obviously refused.

ANNA: He was a very determined man. Loving and tender but determined.

STRANGER: Yet he's now a failure?

ANNA: I wouldn't put it that way. But our hopes were so high. God's kingdom seemed so certain.

STRANGER: And all that is now lost?

CLEOPAS: What can we do without a leader like him?

STRANGER: But surely he must have had a vision of something beyond his death.

CLEOPAS: He believed in the resurrection at the last day, if that's what you mean?

ANNA: There's even a rumor that he has already risen from the dead.

STRANGER: A rumor?

CLEOPAS: Some women went to the grave this morning and were unable to find the body. They returned with stories of angels and an empty tomb.

STRANGER: Did others investigate?

ANNA: Some of the disciples. But no one could find the body.

CLEOPAS: I'm sure someone stole it. Probably the authorities. They couldn't let him rest even in death . . . Ah, here's the waiter. Would you be our guest?

STRANGER: Thank you.

CLEOPAS: I'd recommend the fish.

STRANGER: Alright with me.

CLEOPAS: Three orders of the special.

WAITER: Yes, sir.

CLEOPAS: Now, where were we?

STRANGER: You were saying his body had been stolen.

CLEOPAS: Yes. That's my theory.

STRANGER: Is the body that important?

CLEOPAS: Without a body you can't be a person.

STRANGER: But isn't God able to raise up new life?

CLEOPAS: Without a body?

STRANGER: Without the same body.

CLEOPAS: To me a body is a body.

STRANGER: But do you so limit the power of God?

CLEOPAS: I can't think of life without a body.

STRANGER: But what about a transformed body? One you might not recognize?

CLEOPAS: What are you trying to say?

STRANGER: God is always bringing new life out of despair. The Scriptures are full of it. During the seige of Jerusalem, Jeremiah bought land to show there would be life after the seige. Ezekiel saw a valley of dry bones coming to new life.

CLEOPAS: But those promises applied to the nation.

ANNA: Individuals don't rise from the dead . . . except in the day of resurrection.

WAITER: Your meals. *(He sets down the three dishes of fish, three goblets, a loaf of bread, and a jug of wine.)*

CLEOPAS: Stranger, would you give thanks?

STRANGER: *(as he breaks the loaf)* This is life broken for us. *(as he pours wine into the goblets)* And this is a life poured out for us. And to God be all thanks.

CLEOPAS &
ANNA: To God be all thanks.

ANNA: You believe his death was for some purpose?

STRANGER: God's true servant is often treated harshly. He is brought as a lamb to the slaughter. He is arrested and sentenced and led off to die. And no one cares about his fate.

ANNA: He certainly suffered.

CLEOPAS: But to what purpose? What improvement has it brought?

STRANGER: Has it not shown that love can conquer hate? That the power of God is greater than human evil.

CLEOPAS: I can't say it has. To me it seems so futile.

STRANGER: I can understand your feelings. But don't forget the presence and power of God. *(pause)* However I must be on my way. *(He rises.)*

CLEOPAS: So soon?

STRANGER: Yes. But thank you for your kind hospitality.

CLEOPAS: Perhaps we'll meet again.

STRANGER: We will. *(He leaves.)*

CLEOPAS: A strange person. We never did learn his name.

ANNA: Or where in Galilee he lived. But he was familiar for some reason.

CLEOPAS: He certainly knew the Scriptures.

ANNA: And spoke with such feeling. Didn't it impress you?

CLEOPAS: It reminded me of someone.

ANNA: I had the same feeling. You don't suppose . . .

CLEOPAS: He spoke of resurrection.

ANNA: And changed bodies.

CLEOPAS: And hope.

ANNA: And the power and presence of God.

CLEOPAS: Could it be . . . ?

ANNA: With God all things are possible.

CLEOPAS: *(with still a note of uncertainty)* It must be. We didn't recognize him . . . *(with growing certainty)* but it must be. The way he broke the bread and blessed the wine.

ANNA: It was! It was the risen Christ! Alive in our midst! In a stranger!

CLEOPAS: The women were right! We must share this news with the others . . . without delay. *(They rise and leave.)*

A Strange Meeting

TIME: Easter Sunday afternoon

PLACE: An inn on the road from Jerusalem to Emmaus

CHARACTERS: Cleopas
                Anna: his wife
                A Stranger
                A Waiter

(Cleopas and Anna are seated at a table for four.)

STRANGER: Do you mind if I sit down?

CLEOPAS: Not at all.

STRANGER: The inn's crowded!

CLEOPAS: Yes. *(awkward pause)*

STRANGER: I hope I'm not intruding.

CLEOPAS: No. *(another pause)*

STRANGER: If you'd like to be alone, I can find another spot. *(He begins to rise.)*

CLEOPAS: Stay where you are, stranger. We were just talking over the events of the last few days.

STRANGER: You look dejected.

CLEOPAS: That's an understatement.

STRANGER: Anything I can do to help?

CLEOPAS: Not really.

STRANGER: Where are you from?

CLEOPAS: Galilee.

STRANGER: Up for the Passover?

CLEOPAS: Yes . . . and you?

STRANGER: On my way to Galilee.

ANNA: You were in Jerusalem for the Passover?

STRANGER: Yes.

ANNA: And you don't feel depressed?

STRANGER: About what?

ANNA: About what took place! . . . Those crucifixions!

STRANGER: Nothing new about crucifixions.

ANNA: You weren't disturbed?

STRANGER: I don't enjoy crucifixions, if that's what you mean.

ANNA: You didn't feel the death of Jesus was a great tragedy?

STRANGER: No system of justice is perfect.

CLEOPAS: You're a cool one.

STRANGER: You felt deeply about Jesus?

ANNA: We believed he was a prophet.

STRANGER: Israel's had many prophets.

ANNA: But few, if any, spoke and acted as he did.

STRANGER: Obviously he failed to persuade everyone.

ANNA: Only those blind to his message could refuse.

CLEOPAS: The religious leaders.

STRANGER: But what of the common people?

CLEOPAS: They were for him.

STRANGER: Who shouted for his crucifixion?

CLEOPAS: Mobs can be manipulated.

STRANGER: Yes. But how deep was their loyalty?

ANNA: If they had only known him better.

STRANGER: As you did?

ANNA: As we did.

STRANGER: Yet you feel the crucifixion ended everything?

CLEOPAS: A dead man can't do much.

ANNA: Particularly against Rome.

STRANGER: What did you expect him to do . . . when he was alive, that is?

CLEOPAS: He was going to liberate Israel.

STRANGER: In what way?

ANNA: It didn't matter to us.

CLEOPAS: Some believed it would be by military action . . . some kind of armed insurrection.

STRANGER: From what I've heard, he didn't seem interested in force.

CLEOPAS: He wasn't. And most of those who were looking for it left us long ago. But some thought he might be concealing his plans until the right moment.

ANNA: Others expected God to intervene in some miraculous way from above.

STRANGER: And what kind of kingdom did you expect?

ANNA: One in which there would be freedom to live and worship without oppression.

STRANGER: You're not free to worship and serve God?

CLEOPAS: With the Temple in the hands of traitors and hypocrites?

STRANGER: Yes. I understand he was critical of religious hypocrisy.

CLEOPAS: *(with glee)* You should have heard him . . . those blistering words against the scribes and Pharisees.

STRANGER: But I understand he also said, "Except your righteousness exceed the righteousness of the scribe and Pharisee you shall not see the kingdom of God"?

CLEOPAS: *(slowly and somewhat deflated)* Yes, I recall that one.

ANNA: He could be puzzling at times.

CLEOPAS: He would call us to live with moral integrity and then befriend the hated outcast.

ANNA: In order to bring them back to God, of course.

CLEOPAS: But still as if morality made no difference.

ANNA: He believed good and evil alike were loved by God.

CLEOPAS: Most puzzling.

STRANGER: Didn't he give you any warning that he might be put to death? No instruction of what you should do if that took place?

CLEOPAS: He did speak of suffering and death. But we thought that was just a warning that things might not be too easy.

ANNA: He was warned not to go to Jerusalem for this Passover.

STRANGER: He obviously refused.

ANNA: He was a very determined man. Loving and tender but determined.

STRANGER: Yet he's now a failure?

ANNA: I wouldn't put it that way. But our hopes were so high. God's kingdom seemed so certain.

STRANGER: And all that is now lost?

CLEOPAS: What can we do without a leader like him?

STRANGER: But surely he must have had a vision of something beyond his death.

CLEOPAS: He believed in the resurrection at the last day, if that's what you mean?

ANNA: There's even a rumor that he has already risen from the dead.

STRANGER: A rumor?

CLEOPAS: Some women went to the grave this morning and were unable to find the body. They returned with stories of angels and an empty tomb.

STRANGER: Did others investigate?

ANNA: Some of the disciples. But no one could find the body.

CLEOPAS: I'm sure someone stole it. Probably the authorities. They couldn't let him rest even in death . . . Ah, here's the waiter. Would you be our guest?

STRANGER: Thank you.

CLEOPAS: I'd recommend the fish.

STRANGER: Alright with me.

CLEOPAS: Three orders of the special.

WAITER: Yes, sir.

CLEOPAS: Now, where were we?

STRANGER: You were saying his body had been stolen.

CLEOPAS: Yes. That's my theory.

STRANGER: Is the body that important?

CLEOPAS: Without a body you can't be a person.

STRANGER: But isn't God able to raise up new life?

CLEOPAS: Without a body?

STRANGER: Without the same body.

CLEOPAS: To me a body is a body.

STRANGER: But do you so limit the power of God?

CLEOPAS: I can't think of life without a body.

STRANGER: But what about a transformed body? One you might not recognize?

CLEOPAS: What are you trying to say?

STRANGER: God is always bringing new life out of despair. The Scriptures are full of it. During the seige of Jerusalem, Jeremiah bought land to show there would be life after the seige. Ezekiel saw a valley of dry bones coming to new life.

CLEOPAS: But those promises applied to the nation.

ANNA: Individuals don't rise from the dead . . . except in the day of resurrection.

WAITER: Your meals. *(He sets down the three dishes of fish, three goblets, a loaf of bread, and a jug of wine.)*

CLEOPAS: Stranger, would you give thanks?

STRANGER: *(as he breaks the loaf)* This is life broken for us. *(as he pours wine into the goblets)* And this is a life poured out for us. And to God be all thanks.

CLEOPAS &
ANNA: To God be all thanks.

ANNA: You believe his death was for some purpose?

STRANGER: God's true servant is often treated harshly. He is brought as a lamb to the slaughter. He is arrested and sentenced and led off to die. And no one cares about his fate.

ANNA: He certainly suffered.

CLEOPAS: But to what purpose? What improvement has it brought?

STRANGER: Has it not shown that love can conquer hate? That the power of God is greater than human evil.

CLEOPAS: I can't say it has. To me it seems so futile.

STRANGER: I can understand your feelings. But don't forget the presence and power of God. *(pause)* However I must be on my way. *(He rises.)*

CLEOPAS: So soon?

STRANGER: Yes. But thank you for your kind hospitality.

CLEOPAS: Perhaps we'll meet again.

STRANGER: We will. *(He leaves.)*

CLEOPAS: A strange person. We never did learn his name.

ANNA: Or where in Galilee he lived. But he was familiar for some reason.

CLEOPAS: He certainly knew the Scriptures.

ANNA: And spoke with such feeling. Didn't it impress you?

CLEOPAS: It reminded me of someone.

ANNA: I had the same feeling. You don't suppose . . .

CLEOPAS: He spoke of resurrection.

ANNA: And changed bodies.

CLEOPAS: And hope.

ANNA: And the power and presence of God.

CLEOPAS: Could it be . . . ?

ANNA: With God all things are possible.

CLEOPAS: *(with still a note of uncertainty)* It must be. We didn't recognize him . . . *(with growing certainty)* but it must be. The way he broke the bread and blessed the wine.

ANNA: It was! It was the risen Christ! Alive in our midst! In a stranger!

CLEOPAS: The women were right! We must share this news with the others . . . without delay. *(They rise and leave.)*

A Day on the Soapbox

TIME: The day of Pentecost

PLACE: A public square

CHARACTERS: Abner: a bystander, uncouth, flippant
                  Silas: a bystander, cynical
                  Festus: a bystander, searching
                  Peter

(The three bystanders are looking toward the back of the chancel from the chancel steps.)

ABNER: They must be crazy. I've never seen such nonsense.

SILAS: Religious fanatics!

FESTUS: Quite puzzling.

ABNER: Too much cheap wine.

PETER: *(entering the chancel area)* Wait a minute!

ABNER: They're drunk.

PETER: *(standing on a short wooden crate or its equivalent)* Drunk? Whoever heard of anyone getting drunk this early in the morning?

ABNER: Old pop, here. *(laughter)*

PETER: These people aren't drunk. This is what the prophet Joel promised years ago.

SILAS: Never heard of Joel!

PETER: I can't be responsible for your ignorance.

ABNER: You tell him, preacher!

PETER: Joel promised God would one day pour out his spirit on all flesh.   [*Joel 2:28*]

SILAS: You must be joking. Any self-respecting deity would be more careful.

ABNER: On all flesh? Even old pop? He hasn't been sober for forty years.

PETER: Joel was speaking of all peoples. God isn't only the God of Palestinian Jews. He's the God of the whole world.

SILAS: Sounds noble but people don't respond to that. They need to look down on other people. They can't believe everyone is equal in the sight of God.

PETER: It may be difficult to accept but it's the truth.

ABNER: Next you'll tell us God will pour out his spirit on women and young people.

PETER: Yes!
Your sons and your daughters shall [preach], . . .
    and your young men shall see visions.   [*Joel 2:28*]

ABNER: Just let me catch my wife or kids taking up this preaching bit.

FESTUS: And what about slaves?

PETER: And on my menservants and my maidservants in those days I will pour out my spirit; and they shall prophesy.   [*Joel 2:29*]

SILAS: You really are a dreamer.

FESTUS: Why such a change after all these years? If God wanted to speak through women and young people and slaves, why didn't he do it long before this?

PETER: He did. Have you never heard of Deborah, the youthful Jeremiah, or the slave Aaron?

SILAS: Then what's so new?

PETER: Our realization that God is greater than we have imagined!

FESTUS: But must there be so much emotional excitement?

PETER: Everyone needs some emotional warmth.

FESTUS: But emotions can get out of hand. People can do strange things when they let their feelings run wild.

PETER: They can also do strange things when they become all brain and lose their compassion. These people are joyful. They've experienced the loving presence and power of God. They believe Jesus Christ is their living Lord.

SILAS: Nonsense! I was at that crucifixion. Jesus died. He's had it!

PETER: He died but he hasn't had it.

SILAS: Where is he then?

ABNER: Yeh. If he's alive, let him come out of hiding.

PETER: He's alive in a different sense. He lives by the power of God. He lives in our lives.

SILAS: *(with sarcasm)* And he's responsible for this religious revival?

PETER: Yes. And it's open to all.

FESTUS: I wish I could be so optimistic. We need more than this to solve the mess we're in. We need someone to rid us of these oppressive Romans.

ABNER: And the religious phoneys.

SILAS: To say nothing of the respectable crooks.

PETER: It's easy to place all the blame on others. We all share blame. We too can be greedy and distrustful, on the look out for number one.

ABNER: I take only what's coming to me.

FESTUS: Compared with the big time crooks, we're snow white.

SILAS: The only way to survive in this rat race is to look out for number one.

PETER: You're no different from the people you criticize. If you had the chance, you'd be just as corrupt.

SILAS: Why not? It's time we got our share.

PETER: And with that attitude you expect to build a better world?

ABNER: To blazes with a better world. As long as I get what I want.

PETER: And so say the Romans, and the religious phoneys, and the tax collectors.

FESTUS: You have the perfect solution?

PETER: I'd start by recognizing that we're part of the problem!

FESTUS: And then what?

PETER: Open ourselves to God. Allow him to change our attitude.

SILAS: And the world will be changed overnight.

PETER: I didn't say that. I'm not promising instant paradise. But the first step is to be honest with ourselves.

SILAS: It's a smooth con game — to keep people distracted. If we worry about our own behavior we'll never get to the root of the trouble.

PETER: What's the root of the trouble if it isn't people like you and me?

SILAS: We don't count. It's people with power who corrupt the world.

PETER: And how will you solve that problem?

SILAS: By getting rid of such people.

PETER: And replace them with whom?

SILAS: The common people.

PETER: Like you?

SILAS: Yes.

PETER: Who have the same attitudes?

SILAS: No. I intend to get a fair deal for everyone.

PETER: I wish you success. But if you don't realize you too can be corrupted, you're terribly naive.

FESTUS: But can you guarantee your spirit filled persons will be any better?

PETER: They won't be perfect. No one is. But if one is aware of one's own weakness, open to God's grace, and sensitive to the needs of other people, there's hope for improvement.

SILAS: That kind of person would never last long in the power struggle.

PETER: I hope you're wrong.

SILAS: I know I'm right.

FESTUS: I'm not so sure. The preacher may have a point. It's easy to criticize. Much more difficult to do something constructive.

SILAS: Like having a religious conversion? Not for me. I want to face reality; not run away from it.

PETER: I'm not asking you to run away. I'm asking you to face up to your real self.

SILAS: And become a convert.

PETER: I'd rather say open yourself to God's renewing grace.

SILAS: I don't need anybody's help.

PETER: If you don't, you're a rare person.

SILAS: You know what I mean.

PETER: No. I don't. You think turning to God for help is beneath your dignity.

SILAS: It's a crutch. I want to stand on my own feet.

PETER: Listen! Are you dependent upon food and water and air?

SILAS: Of course.

PETER: Why don't you stand on your own feet and give them up?

SILAS: You keep twisting my words.

PETER: I'm not. We're all dependent upon other things and other people. Standing on one's own feet doesn't mean surviving in haughty independence.

SILAS: You can't deny that people use religion as an escape from responsibility.

PETER: Some do. But that's not what I'm promoting. Accept responsibility for yourself. But realize you can't exist on your own. Live in the strength of God's gracious spirit.

SILAS: I still think it's an evasion. What effect will it have on practical matters . . . such as getting rid of Roman oppressors?

PETER: It's not so much a question of when as how.

SILAS: That's what I mean! More evasion! Always evasion!

PETER: Unless you clarify your means, you'll never reach your goal.

SILAS: Alright then. How? I say we should use force.

PETER: Like the Zealots?

SILAS: Along that line.

PETER: But it's been tried. And thousands have died.

SILAS: Thousands are dying under the present oppression.

PETER: I doubt violence will bring the solution you seek.

SILAS: You can't change this evil world in any other way.

PETER: It's difficult.

SILAS: I'd say impossible.

PETER: There may come a time when . . .

SILAS: *(cutting him off)* And in the meantime we take whatever's thrown at us.

PETER: It depends upon how we take it. With despair or hope, with resignation or creative purpose.

SILAS: You're losing me.

FESTUS: I'm having some difficulty too. You're not denying the power structures need change.

PETER: Not at all. Some of them need to be **destroyed**. But we need to realize our limitations. And we should remember that if we had the power to change the system, we in turn might abuse **our** power and become new oppressors.

FESTUS: You seem to be saying the most effective liberation comes as people are set free from personal bondage by the spirit of God.

PETER: Can you think of any way in which the world can be just and merciful without a change in the hearts and attitudes of people?

SILAS: With the right leaders . . .

PETER: *(cutting in)* You would force people to be righteous?

SILAS: Not exactly. But we'd remove the tyrants.

PETER: Utopian schemes which ignore personal integrity end in tyranny.

SILAS: And I say your message is as Utopian as any other.

FESTUS: I'd like to chat some more with you about this.

PETER: Any time. *(to Silas)* And how about you?

SILAS: Not for me. I'll admit the solution isn't easy. But your talk about the power of God's spirit isn't for me. For good or ill, I'll struggle on my own. *(He walks down the aisle and out of the church.)*

A Day on the Soapbox

TIME: The day of Pentecost

PLACE: A public square

CHARACTERS: Abner: a bystander, uncouth, flippant
                    Silas: a bystander, cynical
                    Festus: a bystander, searching
                    Peter

(The three bystanders are looking toward the back of the chancel from the chancel steps.)

ABNER: They must be crazy. I've never seen such nonsense.

SILAS: Religious fanatics!

FESTUS: Quite puzzling.

ABNER: Too much cheap wine.

PETER: *(entering the chancel area)* Wait a minute!

ABNER: They're drunk.

PETER: *(standing on a short wooden crate or its equivalent)* Drunk? Whoever heard of anyone getting drunk this early in the morning?

ABNER: Old pop, here. *(laughter)*

PETER: These people aren't drunk. This is what the prophet Joel promised years ago.

SILAS: Never heard of Joel!

PETER: I can't be responsible for your ignorance.

ABNER: You tell him, preacher!

PETER: Joel promised God would one day pour out his spirit on all flesh.   *[Joel 2:28]*

SILAS: You must be joking. Any self-respecting deity would be more careful.

ABNER: On all flesh? Even old pop? He hasn't been sober for forty years.

PETER: Joel was speaking of all peoples. God isn't only the God of Palestinian Jews. He's the God of the whole world.

SILAS: Sounds noble but people don't respond to that. They need to look down on other people. They can't believe everyone is equal in the sight of God.

PETER: It may be difficult to accept but it's the truth.

ABNER: Next you'll tell us God will pour out his spirit on women and young people.

PETER: Yes!
Your sons and your daughters shall [preach], . . .
    and your young men shall see visions.   *[Joel 2:28]*

ABNER: Just let me catch my wife or kids taking up this preaching bit.

FESTUS: And what about slaves?

PETER: And on my menservants and my maidservants in those days I will pour out my spirit; and they shall prophesy.   *[Joel 2:29]*

SILAS: You really are a dreamer.

FESTUS: Why such a change after all these years? If God wanted to speak through women and young people and slaves, why didn't he do it long before this?

PETER: He did. Have you never heard of Deborah, the youthful Jeremiah, or the slave Aaron?

SILAS: Then what's so new?

PETER: Our realization that God is greater than we have imagined!

FESTUS: But must there be so much emotional excitement?

PETER: Everyone needs some emotional warmth.

FESTUS: But emotions can get out of hand. People can do strange things when they let their feelings run wild.

PETER: They can also do strange things when they become all brain and lose their compassion. These people are joyful. They've experienced the loving presence and power of God. They believe Jesus Christ is their living Lord.

SILAS: Nonsense! I was at that crucifixion. Jesus died. He's had it!

PETER: He died but he hasn't had it.

SILAS: Where is he then?

ABNER: Yeh. If he's alive, let him come out of hiding.

PETER: He's alive in a different sense. He lives by the power of God. He lives in our lives.

SILAS: *(with sarcasm)* And he's responsible for this religious revival?

PETER: Yes. And it's open to all.

FESTUS: I wish I could be so optimistic. We need more than this to solve the mess we're in. We need someone to rid us of these oppressive Romans.

ABNER: And the religious phoneys.

SILAS: To say nothing of the respectable crooks.

PETER: It's easy to place all the blame on others. We all share blame. We too can be greedy and distrustful, on the look out for number one.

ABNER: I take only what's coming to me.

FESTUS: Compared with the big time crooks, we're snow white.

SILAS: The only way to survive in this rat race **is** to look out for number one.

PETER: You're no different from the people you criticize. If you had the chance, you'd be just as corrupt.

SILAS: Why not? It's time we got our share.

PETER: And with that attitude you expect to build a better world?

ABNER: To blazes with a better world. As long as I get what I want.

PETER: And so say the Romans, and the religious phoneys, and the tax collectors.

FESTUS: You have the perfect solution?

PETER: I'd start by recognizing that we're part of the problem!

FESTUS: And then what?

PETER: Open ourselves to God. Allow him to change our attitude.

SILAS: And the world will be changed overnight.

PETER: I didn't say that. I'm not promising instant paradise. But the first step is to be honest with ourselves.

SILAS: It's a smooth con game — to keep people distracted. If we worry about our own behavior we'll never get to the root of the trouble.

PETER: What's the root of the trouble if it isn't people like you and me?

SILAS: We don't count. It's people with power who corrupt the world.

PETER: And how will you solve that problem?

SILAS: By getting rid of such people.

PETER: And replace them with whom?

SILAS: The common people.

PETER: Like you?

SILAS: Yes.

PETER: Who have the same attitudes?

SILAS: No. I intend to get a fair deal for everyone.

PETER: I wish you success. But if you don't realize you too can be corrupted, you're terribly naive.

FESTUS: But can you guarantee your spirit filled persons will be any better?

PETER: They won't be perfect. No one is. But if one is aware of one's own weakness, open to God's grace, and sensitive to the needs of other people, there's hope for improvement.

SILAS: That kind of person would never last long in the power struggle.

PETER: I hope you're wrong.

SILAS: I know I'm right.

FESTUS: I'm not so sure. The preacher may have a point. It's easy to criticize. Much more difficult to do something constructive.

SILAS: Like having a religious conversion? Not for me. I want to face reality; not run away from it.

PETER: I'm not asking you to run away. I'm asking you to face up to your real self.

SILAS: And become a convert.

PETER: I'd rather say open yourself to God's renewing grace.

SILAS: I don't need anybody's help.

PETER: If you don't, you're a rare person.

SILAS: You know what I mean.

PETER: No. I don't. You think turning to God for help is beneath your dignity.

SILAS: It's a crutch. I want to stand on my own feet.

PETER: Listen! Are you dependent upon food and water and air?

SILAS: Of course.

PETER: Why don't you stand on your own feet and give them up?

SILAS: You keep twisting my words.

PETER: I'm not. We're all dependent upon other things and other people. Standing on one's own feet doesn't mean surviving in haughty independence.

SILAS: You can't deny that people use religion as an escape from responsibility.

PETER: Some do. But that's not what I'm promoting. Accept responsibility for yourself. But realize you can't exist on your own. Live in the strength of God's gracious spirit.

SILAS: I still think it's an evasion. What effect will it have on practical matters . . . such as getting rid of Roman oppressors?

PETER: It's not so much a question of when as how.

SILAS: That's what I mean! More evasion! Always evasion!

PETER: Unless you clarify your means, you'll never reach your goal.

SILAS: Alright then. How? I say we should use force.

PETER: Like the Zealots?

SILAS: Along that line.

PETER: But it's been tried. And thousands have died.

SILAS: Thousands are dying under the present oppression.

PETER: I doubt violence will bring the solution you seek.

SILAS: You can't change this evil world in any other way.

PETER: It's difficult.

SILAS: I'd say impossible.

PETER: There may come a time when . . .

SILAS: *(cutting him off)* And in the meantime we take whatever's thrown at us.

PETER: It depends upon how we take it. With despair or hope, with resignation or creative purpose.

SILAS: You're losing me.

FESTUS: I'm having some difficulty too. You're not denying the power structures need change.

PETER: Not at all. Some of them need to be **destroyed**. But we need to realize our limitations. And we should remember that if we had the power to change the system, we in turn might abuse **our** power and become new oppressors.

FESTUS: You seem to be saying the most effective liberation comes as people are set free from personal bondage by the spirit of God.

PETER: Can you think of any way in which the world can be just and merciful without a change in the hearts and attitudes of people?

SILAS: With the right leaders . . .

PETER: *(cutting in)* You would force people to be righteous?

SILAS: Not exactly. But we'd remove the tyrants.

PETER: Utopian schemes which ignore personal integrity end in tyranny.

SILAS: And I say your message is as Utopian as any other.

FESTUS: I'd like to chat some more with you about this.

PETER: Any time. *(to Silas)* And how about you?

SILAS: Not for me. I'll admit the solution isn't easy. But your talk about the power of God's spirit isn't for me. For good or ill, I'll struggle on my own. *(He walks down the aisle and out of the church.)*

A Day on the Soapbox

TIME: The day of Pentecost

PLACE: A public square

CHARACTERS: Abner: a bystander, uncouth, flippant
                  Silas: a bystander, cynical
                  Festus: a bystander, searching
                  Peter

(The three bystanders are looking toward the back of the chancel from the chancel steps.)

ABNER: They must be crazy. I've never seen such nonsense.

SILAS: Religious fanatics!

FESTUS: Quite puzzling.

ABNER: Too much cheap wine.

PETER: *(entering the chancel area)* Wait a minute!

ABNER: They're drunk.

PETER: *(standing on a short wooden crate or its equivalent)* Drunk? Whoever heard of anyone getting drunk this early in the morning?

ABNER: Old pop, here. *(laughter)*

PETER: These people aren't drunk. This is what the prophet Joel promised years ago.

SILAS: Never heard of Joel!

PETER: I can't be responsible for your ignorance.

ABNER: You tell him, preacher!

PETER: Joel promised God would one day pour out his spirit on all flesh.   *[Joel 2:28]*

SILAS: You must be joking. Any self-respecting deity would be more careful.

ABNER: On all flesh? Even old pop? He hasn't been sober for forty years.

PETER: Joel was speaking of all peoples. God isn't only the God of Palestinian Jews. He's the God of the whole world.

SILAS: Sounds noble but people don't respond to that. They need to look down on other people. They can't believe everyone is equal in the sight of God.

PETER: It may be difficult to accept but it's the truth.

ABNER: Next you'll tell us God will pour out his spirit on women and young people.

PETER: Yes!
Your sons and your daughters shall [preach], . . .
    and your young men shall see visions.   *[Joel 2:28]*

ABNER: Just let me catch my wife or kids taking up this preaching bit.

FESTUS: And what about slaves?

PETER: And on my menservants and my maidservants in those days I will pour out my spirit; and they shall prophesy.   *[Joel 2:29]*

SILAS: You really are a dreamer.

FESTUS: Why such a change after all these years? If God wanted to speak through women and young people and slaves, why didn't he do it long before this?

PETER: He did. Have you never heard of Deborah, the youthful Jeremiah, or the slave Aaron?

SILAS: Then what's so new?

PETER: Our realization that God is greater than we have imagined!

FESTUS: But must there be so much emotional excitement?

PETER: Everyone needs some emotional warmth.

FESTUS: But emotions can get out of hand. People can do strange things when they let their feelings run wild.

PETER: They can also do strange things when they become all brain and lose their compassion. These people are joyful. They've experienced the loving presence and power of God. They believe Jesus Christ is their living Lord.

SILAS: Nonsense! I was at that crucifixion. Jesus died. He's had it!

PETER: He died but he hasn't had it.

SILAS: Where is he then?

ABNER: Yeh. If he's alive, let him come out of hiding.

PETER: He's alive in a different sense. He lives by the power of God. He lives in our lives.

SILAS: *(with sarcasm)* And he's responsible for this religious revival?

PETER: Yes. And it's open to all.

FESTUS: I wish I could be so optimistic. We need more than this to solve the mess we're in. We need someone to rid us of these oppressive Romans.

ABNER: And the religious phoneys.

SILAS: To say nothing of the respectable crooks.

PETER: It's easy to place all the blame on others. We all share blame. We too can be greedy and distrustful, on the look out for number one.

ABNER: I take only what's coming to me.

FESTUS: Compared with the big time crooks, we're snow white.

SILAS: The only way to survive in this rat race is to look out for number one.

PETER: You're no different from the people you criticize. If you had the chance, you'd be just as corrupt.

SILAS: Why not? It's time we got our share.

PETER: And with that attitude you expect to build a better world?

ABNER: To blazes with a better world. As long as I get what I want.

PETER: And so say the Romans, and the religious phoneys, and the tax collectors.

FESTUS: You have the perfect solution?

PETER: I'd start by recognizing that we're part of the problem!

FESTUS: And then what?

PETER: Open ourselves to God. Allow him to change our attitude.

SILAS: And the world will be changed overnight.

PETER: I didn't say that. I'm not promising instant paradise. But the first step is to be honest with ourselves.

SILAS: It's a smooth con game — to keep people distracted. If we worry about our own behavior we'll never get to the root of the trouble.

PETER: What's the root of the trouble if it isn't people like you and me?

SILAS: We don't count. It's people with power who corrupt the world.

PETER: And how will you solve that problem?

SILAS: By getting rid of such people.

PETER: And replace them with whom?

SILAS: The common people.

PETER: Like you?

SILAS: Yes.

PETER: Who have the same attitudes?

SILAS: No. I intend to get a fair deal for everyone.

PETER: I wish you success. But if you don't realize you too can be corrupted, you're terribly naive.

FESTUS: But can you guarantee your spirit filled persons will be any better?

PETER: They won't be perfect. No one is. But if one is aware of one's own weakness, open to God's grace, and sensitive to the needs of other people, there's hope for improvement.

SILAS: That kind of person would never last long in the power struggle.

PETER: I hope you're wrong.

SILAS: I know I'm right.

FESTUS: I'm not so sure. The preacher may have a point. It's easy to criticize. Much more difficult to do something constructive.

SILAS: Like having a religious conversion? Not for me. I want to face reality; not run away from it.

PETER: I'm not asking you to run away. I'm asking you to face up to your real self.

SILAS: And become a convert.

PETER: I'd rather say open yourself to God's renewing grace.

SILAS: I don't need anybody's help.

PETER: If you don't, you're a rare person.

SILAS: You know what I mean.

PETER: No. I don't. You think turning to God for help is beneath your dignity.

SILAS: It's a crutch. I want to stand on my own feet.

PETER: Listen! Are you dependent upon food and water and air?

SILAS: Of course.

PETER: Why don't you stand on your own feet and give them up?

SILAS: You keep twisting my words.

PETER: I'm not. We're all dependent upon other things and other people. Standing on one's own feet doesn't mean surviving in haughty independence.

SILAS: You can't deny that people use religion as an escape from responsibility.

PETER: Some do. But that's not what I'm promoting. Accept responsibility for yourself. But realize you can't exist on your own. Live in the strength of God's gracious spirit.

SILAS: I still think it's an evasion. What effect will it have on practical matters . . . such as getting rid of Roman oppressors?

PETER: It's not so much a question of when as how.

SILAS: That's what I mean! More evasion! Always evasion!

PETER: Unless you clarify your means, you'll never reach your goal.

SILAS: Alright then. How? I say we should use force.

PETER: Like the Zealots?

SILAS: Along that line.

PETER: But it's been tried. And thousands have died.

SILAS: Thousands are dying under the present oppression.

PETER: I doubt violence will bring the solution you seek.

SILAS: You can't change this evil world in any other way.

PETER: It's difficult.

SILAS: I'd say impossible.

PETER: There may come a time when . . .

SILAS: *(cutting him off)* And in the meantime we take whatever's thrown at us.

PETER: It depends upon how we take it. With despair or hope, with resignation or creative purpose.

SILAS: You're losing me.

FESTUS: I'm having some difficulty too. You're not denying the power structures need change.

PETER: Not at all. Some of them need to be **destroyed**. But we need to realize our limitations. And we should remember that if we had the power to change the system, we in turn might abuse **our** power and become new oppressors.

FESTUS: You seem to be saying the most effective liberation comes as people are set free from personal bondage by the spirit of God.

PETER: Can you think of any way in which the world can be just and merciful without a change in the hearts and attitudes of people?

SILAS: With the right leaders . . .

PETER: *(cutting in)* You would force people to be righteous?

SILAS: Not exactly. But we'd remove the tyrants.

PETER: Utopian schemes which ignore personal integrity end in tyranny.

SILAS: And I say your message is as Utopian as any other.

FESTUS: I'd like to chat some more with you about this.

PETER: Any time. *(to Silas)* And how about you?

SILAS: Not for me. I'll admit the solution isn't easy. But your talk about the power of God's spirit isn't for me. For good or ill, I'll struggle on my own. *(He walks down the aisle and out of the church.)*

A Day on the Soapbox

TIME: The day of Pentecost

PLACE: A public square

CHARACTERS: Abner: a bystander, uncouth, flippant

                  Silas: a bystander, cynical

                  Festus: a bystander, searching

                  Peter

(The three bystanders are looking toward the back of the chancel from the chancel steps.)

ABNER: They must be crazy. I've never seen such nonsense.

SILAS: Religious fanatics!

FESTUS: Quite puzzling.

ABNER: Too much cheap wine.

PETER: *(entering the chancel area)* Wait a minute!

ABNER: They're drunk.

PETER: *(standing on a short wooden crate or its equivalent)* Drunk? Whoever heard of anyone getting drunk this early in the morning?

ABNER: Old pop, here. *(laughter)*

PETER: These people aren't drunk. This is what the prophet Joel promised years ago.

SILAS: Never heard of Joel!

PETER: I can't be responsible for your ignorance.

ABNER: You tell him, preacher!

PETER: Joel promised God would one day pour out his spirit on all flesh.   [*Joel 2:28*]

SILAS: You must be joking. Any self-respecting deity would be more careful.

ABNER: On all flesh? Even old pop? He hasn't been sober for forty years.

PETER: Joel was speaking of all peoples. God isn't only the God of Palestinian Jews. He's the God of the whole world.

SILAS: Sounds noble but people don't respond to that. They need to look down on other people. They can't believe everyone is equal in the sight of God.

PETER: It may be difficult to accept but it's the truth.

ABNER: Next you'll tell us God will pour out his spirit on women and young people.

PETER: Yes!

            Your sons and your daughters shall [preach], . . .

              and your young men shall see visions.   [*Joel 2:28*]

ABNER: Just let me catch my wife or kids taking up this preaching bit.

FESTUS: And what about slaves?

PETER: And on my menservants and my maidservants in those days I will pour out my spirit; and they shall prophesy.   [*Joel 2:29*]

SILAS: You really are a dreamer.

FESTUS: Why such a change after all these years? If God wanted to speak through women and young people and slaves, why didn't he do it long before this?

PETER: He did. Have you never heard of Deborah, the youthful Jeremiah, or the slave Aaron?

SILAS: Then what's so new?

PETER: Our realization that God is greater than we have imagined!

FESTUS: But must there be so much emotional excitement?

PETER: Everyone needs some emotional warmth.

FESTUS: But emotions can get out of hand. People can do strange things when they let their feelings run wild.

PETER: They can also do strange things when they become all brain and lose their compassion. These people are joyful. They've experienced the loving presence and power of God. They believe Jesus Christ is their living Lord.

SILAS: Nonsense! I was at that crucifixion. Jesus died. He's had it!

PETER: He died but he hasn't had it.

SILAS: Where is he then?

ABNER: Yeh. If he's alive, let him come out of hiding.

PETER: He's alive in a different sense. He lives by the power of God. He lives in our lives.

SILAS: *(with sarcasm)* And he's responsible for this religious revival?

PETER: Yes. And it's open to all.

FESTUS: I wish I could be so optimistic. We need more than this to solve the mess we're in. We need someone to rid us of these oppressive Romans.

ABNER: And the religious phoneys.

SILAS: To say nothing of the respectable crooks.

PETER: It's easy to place all the blame on others. We all share blame. We too can be greedy and distrustful, on the look out for number one.

ABNER: I take only what's coming to me.

FESTUS: Compared with the big time crooks, we're snow white.

SILAS: The only way to survive in this rat race is to look out for number one.

PETER: You're no different from the people you criticize. If you had the chance, you'd be just as corrupt.

SILAS: Why not? It's time we got our share.

PETER: And with that attitude you expect to build a better world?

ABNER: To blazes with a better world. As long as I get what I want.

PETER: And so say the Romans, and the religious phoneys, and the tax collectors.

FESTUS: You have the perfect solution?

PETER: I'd start by recognizing that we're part of the problem!

FESTUS: And then what?

PETER: Open ourselves to God. Allow him to change our attitude.

SILAS: And the world will be changed overnight.

PETER: I didn't say that. I'm not promising instant paradise. But the first step is to be honest with ourselves.

SILAS: It's a smooth con game — to keep people distracted. If we worry about our own behavior we'll never get to the root of the trouble.

PETER: What's the root of the trouble if it isn't people like you and me?

SILAS: We don't count. It's people with power who corrupt the world.

PETER: And how will you solve that problem?

SILAS: By getting rid of such people.

PETER: And replace them with whom?

SILAS: The common people.

PETER: Like you?

SILAS: Yes.

PETER: Who have the same attitudes?

SILAS: No. I intend to get a fair deal for everyone.

PETER: I wish you success. But if you don't realize you too can be corrupted, you're terribly naive.

FESTUS: But can you guarantee your spirit filled persons will be any better?

PETER: They won't be perfect. No one is. But if one is aware of one's own weakness, open to God's grace, and sensitive to the needs of other people, there's hope for improvement.

SILAS: That kind of person would never last long in the power struggle.

PETER: I hope you're wrong.

SILAS: I know I'm right.

FESTUS: I'm not so sure. The preacher may have a point. It's easy to criticize. Much more difficult to do something constructive.

SILAS: Like having a religious conversion? Not for me. I want to face reality; not run away from it.

PETER: I'm not asking you to run away. I'm asking you to face up to your real self.

SILAS: And become a convert.

PETER: I'd rather say open yourself to God's renewing grace.

SILAS: I don't need anybody's help.

PETER: If you don't, you're a rare person.

SILAS: You know what I mean.

PETER: No. I don't. You think turning to God for help is beneath your dignity.

SILAS: It's a crutch. I want to stand on my own feet.

PETER: Listen! Are you dependent upon food and water and air?

SILAS: Of course.

PETER: Why don't you stand on your own feet and give them up?

SILAS: You keep twisting my words.

PETER: I'm not. We're all dependent upon other things and other people. Standing on one's own feet doesn't mean surviving in haughty independence.

SILAS: You can't deny that people use religion as an escape from responsibility.

PETER: Some do. But that's not what I'm promoting. Accept responsibility for yourself. But realize you can't exist on your own. Live in the strength of God's gracious spirit.

SILAS: I still think it's an evasion. What effect will it have on practical matters . . . such as getting rid of Roman oppressors?

PETER: It's not so much a question of when as how.

SILAS: That's what I mean! More evasion! Always evasion!

PETER: Unless you clarify your means, you'll never reach your goal.

SILAS: Alright then. How? I say we should use force.

PETER: Like the Zealots?

SILAS:	Along that line.
PETER:	But it's been tried. And thousands have died.
SILAS:	Thousands are dying under the present oppression.
PETER:	I doubt violence will bring the solution you seek.
SILAS:	You can't change this evil world in any other way.
PETER:	It's difficult.
SILAS:	I'd say impossible.
PETER:	There may come a time when . . .
SILAS:	*(cutting him off)* And in the meantime we take whatever's thrown at us.
PETER:	It depends upon how we take it. With despair or hope, with resignation or creative purpose.
SILAS:	You're losing me.
FESTUS:	I'm having some difficulty too. You're not denying the power structures need change.
PETER:	Not at all. Some of them need to be **destroyed**. But we need to realize our limitations. And we should remember that if we had the power to change the system, we in turn might abuse **our** power and become new oppressors.
FESTUS:	You seem to be saying the most effective liberation comes as people are set free from personal bondage by the spirit of God.
PETER:	Can you think of any way in which the world can be just and merciful without a change in the hearts and attitudes of people?
SILAS:	With the right leaders . . .
PETER:	*(cutting in)* You would force people to be righteous?
SILAS:	Not exactly. But we'd remove the tyrants.
PETER:	Utopian schemes which ignore personal integrity end in tyranny.
SILAS:	And I say your message is as Utopian as any other.
FESTUS:	I'd like to chat some more with you about this.
PETER:	Any time. *(to Silas)* And how about you?
SILAS:	Not for me. I'll admit the solution isn't easy. But your talk about the power of God's spirit isn't for me. For good or ill, I'll struggle on my own. *(He walks down the aisle and out of the church.)*